SEVEN FOUNTAINS OF LOVE

THE CROSS OF CHRIST

THOMAS W. MORRIS, MD

WESTBOW
PRESS®
A DIVISION OF THOMAS NELSON
& ZONDERVAN

WestBow Press books may be ordered through booksellers or by contacting:

WestBow Press
A Division of Thomas Nelson & Zondervan
1663 Liberty Drive
Bloomington, IN 47403
www.westbowpress.com
1 (866) 928-1240

ISBN: 978-1-5127-2180-5 (sc)
ISBN: 978-1-5127-2178-2 (hc)
ISBN: 978-1-5127-2179-9 (e)

Library of Congress Control Number: 2015919587

Print information available on the last page.

WestBow Press rev. date: 12/9/2015

This book is dedicated to Jesus Christ, whose suffering is described within its pages and without whom we could never have known so great salvation. High praise is due to the Father, whose grace sent him to die for humankind, and to the Holy Spirit, who revealed the works of Jesus at the cross.

CONTENTS

ACKNOWLEDGMENTS

I wish to thank my wonderful wife, Tesa, without whose encouragement and support this book would not have been possible.

In addition, I would like to express my appreciation to my daughter and son-in-law, Dee and Buddy Bodiford, for their encouragement and much-needed technical support.

A great big thank you is due to my grand-daughter, Shelby Pierce, for all the help with the computer.

INTRODUCTION

Shortly after noon on April 10, 1912, the great ship *Titanic* slipped from her moorings in Southampton, England, for her maiden voyage to America. She was the largest ship afloat; actually, *Titanic* was the largest movable man-made object ever built up to that time. In addition, this massive ship was considered "unsinkable."

All those on board were said to have been in high spirits as the ship set her course for Cherbourg, France, the first leg of her passage to America. All were oblivious to the impending disaster, which would send approximately 1,500 of the souls on board to a watery grave. In fact, right up until the ship struck the ice, no passenger or crew member had the slightest notion that the "safest ship afloat" would be resting on the floor on the Atlantic Ocean in fewer than five days. It is probably safe to say that even after impact with the giant mass of ice, few of them fully comprehended the magnitude of the catastrophic event that had transpired. Only when the doomed vessel began to list to starboard and word began to circulate as to the extent of the disaster that had befallen *Titanic* did fear begin to seize passenger and crew alike.

Although *Titanic* had received at least six messages warning her of icebergs in her vicinity, the ship never reduced speed but continued to maintain twenty-two knots (twenty-five miles per hour), just two knots short of her maximum speed of twenty-four knots (twenty-eight miles per hour).

There is ample reason to suspect that our great country, the United States of America, may be on a collision course with the unthinkable, much like *Titanic*. Our great "ship of state" has been considered unsinkable; only a few short years ago, very few would have entertained any notion to the contrary. However, events of the recent past, especially since September 11, 2001, have seriously eroded the confidence of Americans. With 9/11 came the threat to national security, which was deposited on the doorstep of the nation with such emphasis that even the most passive were shaken to attention. Not since Pearl Harbor had the United States been treated with such blatant disdain. A relatively small group of terrorists contemptuously threw the gauntlet at the feet of the most powerful nation on earth and dared her to take up the challenge. This country answered the affront to her sovereignty, responding with money, guns, and the blood of her sons and daughters, but the risk today remains as real as it was in 2001.

If the threat to national security were limited to Islamic terrorism, the situation might not appear so bad. Add to the pot concerns over an unhealthy economy, and the stew begins to thicken. The daily news calls for us to stir in a dash of societal breakdown, including school shootings, racial discontent, family disintegration, and suicide, all of which seems to have increased exponentially over the past few years.

As with the captain and crew of the *Titanic*, those who were elected to guide this nation can never say they were not warned of impending disaster. Health threats are commonplace; the economy is in shambles (we are approaching the point where we will not be able to pay the interest on the national debt); our infrastructure is collapsing; and we are even now beginning to feel the effects of cyber warfare. And as if this were not enough, there are concerns over biological, chemical, and nuclear weapons that remain viable options for the terrorists.

However, the present leadership of this country appears more concerned with reelection than with the future of the nation and therefore remains deadlocked much of the time. It is extremely unlikely that, under the present circumstances, any conventional solutions will be effective in bringing about positive change.

The citizens of this nation, throughout much of the twentieth century, basked in a sense of security fostered by a long-term position of strength. Though we had enemies during the Cold War, this country held the respect of most nations around the world, both large and small. As of late, however, serious reversals have occurred. Following the Vietnam and Gulf Wars, our prestige declined precipitously. We have lost the respect of many friends and gained greater contempt from our enemies. Though icebergs of every type and description seem to be popping up on the horizon, the leadership of this country seems determined to steer the same course and maintain full speed ahead. They either refuse to acknowledge the dangers or possibly have become so inundated by the sheer volume of the threats that they have become incapacitated. Whatever the reason for the inadequate response, the helm seems to be set, and it appears highly unlikely that a rational solution will be forthcoming from the existing powers in Washington, DC.

In addition to minimizing the iceberg risk, *Titanic* carried too few lifeboats to accommodate the passengers and crew aboard the ship. In view of the incomprehensible determination to spend this nation into unsustainable debt and the seeming ineptitude of her captain and crew in navigating this great ship of state through the twenty-first–century iceberg fields, all passengers aboard can be reasonably assured that the lifeboat count will be inadequate also.

The citizens of this nation seem as powerless to change the course and speed of our great ship as those passengers who were aboard the *Titanic*. However, we do have an advantage. The perils this country faces, though many, are obvious. Unlike the passengers aboard *Titanic*, our icebergs stand clearly before us. The passengers and crew who remained on board *Titanic*, as the last lifeboats made their way into the dark, icy waters of the North Atlantic, began to sing an old Christian hymn, "Nearer My God to Thee."

Those people faced impending death and sought to be near God in heaven. We face only the threat of catastrophe; consequently, if we, as individuals, begin now to sing *Titanic*'s song before disaster strikes, we just might be able to avert disaster. Let us begin, even now, to make "Nearer My God to Thee" the anthem for our lives.

Let us refuse to sail any farther into the unknown darkness of uncharted waters. May we acknowledge God as our pilot and trust to his ability to navigate our ship through this unfamiliar twenty-first-century course. He is the One who loves unconditionally, and he wills to be near those who choose to be near him.

As a nation and as individuals, we need to turn to God. Prior to every war in which this country has been involved, Americans have petitioned almighty God on behalf of the nation and its armed forces. Let it not be said of the present generation that our great civilization perished because we lacked the wisdom to do so. Without him, any upstart with a desire to do so may hold this country and the world hostage. However, even as the enemies of Israel fell before them when they sought God, and as the Axis powers crumbled under the combined forces of the United States and her allies, so will the enemies of today be devastated.

We should pray for our leaders that they would see the need to call the nation to prayer and to seek the Lord's guidance in these turbulent times. But if they should refuse to do so, this in no way relieves the individual of the responsibility to hold this blessed nation up in prayer before the Lord.

No matter what transpires with this world or with the United States, let us not trust for our security to this or any nation, or to our families, or to ourselves. May we resolve to put our confidence in our Lord Jesus Christ. Psalm 91:1–6 reads:

> He who dwells in the secret place of the most high
> shall abide under the shadow of the Almighty.
> I will say of the Lord, "He is my refuge and my
> fortress; my God, in him I will trust." Surely he

shall deliver you from the snare of the fowler and from the perilous pestilence. He shall cover you with his feathers, and under his wings you shall take refuge; his truth shall be your shield and buckler. You shall not be afraid of the terror by night, nor of the arrow that flies by day, nor of the pestilence that walks in darkness, nor of the destruction that lays waste at noon day.

Let us sing in the quiet of our place of prayer "Nearer My God to Thee." It is my opinion that in order to draw near to God, we should begin at the cross, where the precious blood of the Son of God was shed. The reference to the seven fountains of love expressed in the title of this book speaks to the seven sources from which blood flowed from the body of our Lord during the events surrounding his crucifixion. We will begin in the garden of Gethsemane and proceed to the piercing of his side by the Roman soldiers. Everything we need, including salvation and all of our spiritual and physical needs, while on this earth are provided through the cross and the precious blood, which was shed there. This includes protection from those who will do our country harm.

Let us take a fresh look at the cross.

CHAPTER 1

THE CROSS

Not with wisdom of words, lest the cross of
Christ should be made of none effect.
—1 Corinthians 1:17

Approximately two thousand years ago, a young Jewish rabbi
struggled to make his way up a hill called Golgotha, which was
located just outside the city of Jerusalem. The short journey had
been made extremely difficult by the fact that this man had been
beaten by Roman soldiers to a point very near death. In addition,
he was forced to carry a Roman cross—or at least a heavy wooden
crossbeam—to the place where he was to be crucified. Upon reaching
the summit, he was pinned to the cross, one nail through each hand
or wrist and one nail penetrating his overlapped feet. He then hung
there, suspended between heaven and earth, until he was dead. This
was the fulfillment of a sentence handed down by Pontius Pilate,
Roman governor of Judea. It has been said that Pilate was reticent to
give the order to execute, having found no fault in Jesus of Nazareth.
However, at the behest of the Jewish religious hierarchy and in the
interest of keeping the peace in Judea, he had proceeded with the
order to crucify Jesus.

No one on earth could have anticipated the impact that this execution would have upon the world. On that day, a fire was ignited that swept the world of that time, and the blaze, though diminished at times, has continued for two millennia. Following the crucifixion of Jesus, the cross itself would become a symbol of devotion to him, who had died upon it. It came to adorn everything from the spires of great cathedrals throughout the world to the simple jewelry worn by those who have followed him.

In the two thousand–year interval since his death, untold numbers of people from every corner of the globe have assented to follow Jesus. And why not? During his lifetime, he claimed to be the Son of God, who had come from heaven to this earth in order to reveal to those who would hear the message of everlasting life. During his earthly life, he appeared to hold the keys to death, hell, and the grave and to possess the power to bring the believer into fellowship with the Creator. He was a great teacher, he performed great miracles, and most of all, he arose from the dead three days after the events at Golgotha.

Throughout history, many masterful teachers have lived on this earth, and many miracle workers have made astounding claims. A few have alleged that they possessed the power to resurrect the dead, but Jesus is the only one who ever achieved any valid reputation concerning power over death. Not only did he raise more than one from the dead during his ministry, but he also returned to life after his crucifixion.

All of this is well and good, but it is limited to only those who believe. Therefore, it is incumbent upon every individual on earth to seriously consider this question: was that man who walked to the summit of Golgotha and died there actually the Son of God, or was he not? If he was not the Son of God, then Christianity is the greatest falsehood ever conceived. Every cross atop every cathedral and church throughout the world stands as mute testimony to the greatest con ever perpetrated upon humankind. The Bible becomes less valuable than the paper upon which it is printed and should, therefore, be relegated to the trash heap and burned. Some, however, would argue that it should be preserved for its poetic or historical value, further contending that Jesus should be remembered because he was a wonderful teacher. And others would laud him because of the marvelous works he performed during his ministry here on earth.

But Jesus said in John 18:37, "You say rightly that I am a King. For this cause I was born, and for this cause I have come into the world, *that I should bear witness to the truth.* Everyone who is of the truth hears my voice" (emphasis mine). Here, he gives the telling of the truth as his primary reason for having been born. Moreover, in John 14:6, he says, "I am the way, the truth, and the life. No one comes to the Father except through Me" (emphasis mine). This great teacher claims to be the truth incarnate. He claims that he was born to bring truth to this earth. Yet this same one who is the truth said to Caiaphas, the high priest, during his pre-crucifixion trial, "Nevertheless, I say to you, hereafter you will see the Son of Man sitting at the right hand of the Power [God] and coming on the clouds of heaven" (Matthew 26:64). In Mark 14:61–62, the high priest asked Jesus, "Are you the Christ, the Son of the Blessed?" And Jesus answered, "I am," followed by the same words used in the twenty-sixth chapter of Matthew.

This one who claims to have come to earth in order to bring truth into our world also claims to be the Christ, the Son of God. I repeat what I said earlier: if he was not God, then he was a liar, and he can claim no right to having been a great teacher of truth. Indeed, his life should have been spared on the grounds of insanity. No natural man, making the audacious claims that Jesus made during his life on earth, should be honored as a great teacher, miracle worker, or minister. If he was presumptuous enough to call himself the Son of God and brazen enough to tell a Roman governor that his mission on earth was truth, then those who seek the truth should want no part of this man's teaching. Surely, his healing of the sick, casting out demons, and, by all means, raising the dead had to be no more than the work of a master charlatan. Of course, the foregoing is true only if Jesus was not God. What if, however, the young rabbi in question was truly the Son of the almighty God? If he was the Son of God, then all that the Scripture has to say about him is automatically validated. If he is part of the Godhead, which created the earth and gave life to all that lives, then it becomes reasonable that his teachings are all truthful, and his miracles actually occurred as written. Even his resurrection from the dead becomes plausible if he, in truth, is the one who gave life in the first place. If he was God, it then becomes incomprehensible that he would have given his followers unreliable information. He is perfection; therefore, his Word, the Bible, has to be inerrant and must be considered truth.

In addition, that truth tells every lonely, defeated, depressed, and lost soul that God has said, "I will never leave you nor forsake you" (Hebrews 13:5). Herein lies the answer for the individual, the United States of America, and the world. It is here in his presence that we find true, transforming peace. And there is no better place to start than with the greatest expression of his love for humankind: the cross of Christ. No act on his part, from Adam to the present, better exemplifies God's attitude toward humanity than the crucifixion of his Son. John 3:16, the most quoted verse in the Bible, sums it up, clearly acknowledging the love of God as the motivation for the crucifixion of Jesus Christ. God loves humankind with such phenomenal affection that he gave up his only begotten Son, so that if we simply believe that his shed blood paid for our sins, we have eternal life.

It is here at the cross that we first realized the truth of his love and received the eternal salvation that it offered. While this conversion experience is the first step and certainly must be taken in order to grasp a position of everlasting security, it is just that: the first step. It is easy to become fixated here and never pursue the blessings set before us by his wondrous love. By falling into some routine of service, we lose our primary reason for having believed in the beginning, which was and is fellowship with the Father, Son, and Holy Spirit. In this condition, we soon lose the peace and joy that we first encountered with the Lord. While it is relatively simple to restore communion with God, it is easy to become surrounded by others who are walking in the same religious quagmire. And if we are not careful, we then become part of a "body of persons adhering to a particular set of beliefs and practices," which is *Webster's* definition for religion. While I suppose there is nothing inherently wrong with being a part of religion, when that set of beliefs and rituals begins to replace God's love, it should awaken us to the probability that something may be off course. In fact, anything on earth that separates us from the love of God, even to the slightest degree, should set off an alarm, for without his love, everything becomes lifeless and without meaning.

First Corinthians 13:1–3 reads, "Though I speak with the tongues of men and of Angels, but have not love, I have become sounding brass or a clanging cymbal. And though I have the gift of prophecy, and understand all mysteries and all knowledge, and though I have all faith, so that I could remove mountains, but have not love, I am nothing. And though I bestow all my goods to feed the poor, and though I give my body to be burned, but have not love, it profits me nothing." In other words, if I am not experiencing the love that God has for me, and I am not reciprocating with love for him, then nothing that I do counts for anything. All my religious efforts are for naught. Not only are my efforts wasted, but I am, at the same time, missing out on the most glorious experience available to a child of God. As his child, I have the blood-bought right to walk with my heavenly Father. He is my Father; I am his son. Romans 8:15 reads, "For you did not receive the spirit of bondage again to fear, but you received the Spirit of adoption by whom we cry out, Abba [Daddy], Father."

My one and only concern is to introduce anyone who will hear to a loving Father, who offers his heart to whosoever will believe him. He is that same one whose still small voice may be heard above the incessant clamor of this modern world and the façade of religious rhetoric and ritualism. Though he is all-powerful and can easily storm our hearts and minds, he quietly waits for the hopeless soul to call upon him. To that one who may be confused by all the religious requirements, just remember that the thief on the cross at the time of Christ's crucifixion said simply, "Remember me when you come into your kingdom." The response of Jesus to this sincere request is, again, a simple one: "...today you will be with me in Paradise" (Luke 23:42–43). You do not have to wait until your final breath, as was the case with the thief on the cross. Any suffering heart who will call upon him will hear him say, "This day you shall be with me." Not someday or one day in the by-and-by, but this day he will be with you. His purpose in coming to this earth was to reunite each of us with his Father. Let me repeat this for emphasis: his motive is love for you, and his desire is to bring you into a peaceful relationship with the Father and Himself.

There is nothing that you have done and nothing that you have failed to do that can separate you from the love of God, if you desire to receive it. His love awaits your decision and that only. You are the only thing that stands in the way. Your sin does not prohibit you from coming to him, for he has paid the price for every sin that you have committed. He loves every sinner, and there is absolutely no sin that has not been forgiven through his grace.

The importance of coming to know him and his great love cannot be overstated. It is truly a crying shame that right in the middle of religious endeavor, many Christians are unaware of the loving presence of Jesus Christ. Nothing must be allowed to stand in the way of accessing the love of Christ. Whatever the objection, be it great or small, we must be still and allow him to prove himself by waiting calmly and patiently for him. Isaiah 40:31 reads, "But those who wait on the Lord shall renew their strength; they shall mount up with wings like eagles, they shall run and not be weary, they shall walk and not faint." This is true for any Christian who will make the love of God his primary goal. God desires to make himself known to you, and when you begin seriously to seek him, he will make himself available. If you are seeking peace, change your course and seek him; he will give you peace. John 14:27 reads, "Peace I leave with you, My peace I give to you; not as the world gives do I give to you. Let not your heart be troubled, neither let it be afraid." God's peace was of primary importance to the apostle Paul. He opened just about every one of his New Testament letters with a desire for peace for all those who received his correspondence. This was not peace that this world offers, which waxes and wanes with each circumstance or event. In fact, Jesus differentiated between the peace of this world and the peace that he gives in John 14:27. Neither was this just a nice phrase with which Paul chose to begin his letters. This was the peace spoken of in Philippians 4:7, "which surpasses all understanding." This is that same peace that will sustain all those who will appropriate it. How, then, do we access this peace? We simply turn to the Prince of Peace, the one whose coming was heralded by the angels: "Peace on earth, goodwill to men." We should reexamine our faith as we begin again to seek him. If not a Christian, a faith walk with him must be established by asking for his forgiveness and trusting that his blood, which was shed upon the cross, paid the debt for our sins.

Let us return to the cross. The songwriter of old wrote, "The way of the cross leads home." Let us go and see if this is true. I too want to be at home with the Lord, and if we are to proceed, then we must affirm or reaffirm some fundamental truths. My faith in Christ stands because of his faithfulness and his presence with me. Oh yes, I have—on many occasions during my seventy-five years—walked away from him, usually attempting to live within my own capabilities. Failing in all my endeavors and longing for his love, I was inevitably drawn back to him. He never failed to be right there with me, the very moment that I chose to turn around. He always seemed to be happy to welcome me back.

He does not sit on his throne, ready to punish; rather, he welcomes his children home. He is a God of love and chooses to love and be loved. Then the question arises: what about sin? This

7

will be discussed in detail later, but for now, let us rest upon the truth that when we first became believers, we were forgiven for all that we had done. There is no difference when we return to him; he seeks to forgive. He is a loving Father, and when we accept Jesus's sacrifice as atonement for our sins, we are accepted into his household as children. Ephesians 1:3–6 reads, "Blessed be the God and Father of our Lord Jesus Christ, who has blessed us with every spiritual blessing in the heavenly places in Christ, just as He chose us in Him before the foundation of the world, that we should be holy and without blame before Him in love, having predestined us to adoption as sons by Jesus Christ to Himself, according to the good pleasure of His will, to the praise of the glory of His grace, by which *He made us accepted in the Beloved*" (emphasis mine). And let us repeat Romans 8:15–16: "For you did not receive the spirit of bondage again to fear, but you received the Spirit of adoption by whom we cry out, 'Abba, Father.' The Spirit himself bears witness with our spirit that we are the children of God."

We have a Father who loves us enough to have made us all—those of us who believe—his children. He seeks to shower his love upon us, and he has made arrangements so that nothing can separate us from his love—not tribulation, distress, persecution, famine, nakedness, peril, or sword, according to Romans 8:35–37. And in verses 38 and 39 of Romans 8, Paul tells us, "For I am persuaded that neither death nor life, nor angels nor principalities nor powers, nor things present nor things to come, nor height nor depth, nor any other created thing, shall be able to separate us from the love of God which is in Christ Jesus our Lord."

This does not come across as an out-of-touch or vengeful God, does it? We need to begin to stand in our Father's love for us. You may not have experienced an earthly father's love, and at first it may be a little difficult to accept the love of your heavenly Father. But begin to trust his Word and confess this truth, and it will become reality to you. Simply begin to see yourself as his child, and a personal relationship will begin to develop.

Do not allow Satan to interfere. This is his most important project where man is concerned, and he will most assuredly attack on this front. In Revelation 12:10, he is referred to as the accuser. He would like to keep you thinking that your Father seeks to condemn you for even the slightest infraction. Determine that you will no longer allow Satan to get away with this ploy. Quote the Scripture to him, even as Jesus did in the wilderness. He wants to separate you from the love of God, so stand against him with Scripture, which speaks of God's love for you. Openly confess that God loves you and that he forgives your sin.

Common sense tells us that if a child of two or three years of age wanders into a mud hole and soils his or her clothing, the mother of that child does not abandon him or her. Nor does she expect him to go inside and clean himself up; she simply picks him up and washes him clean. She may discipline him, but her love for the child continues, and in a normal setting, no vengeance is involved. Now, this raises an obvious question: if the love of an earthly mother is such that she cannot abandon her child or mistreat her, then how can we believe that our heavenly Father would abandon or mistreat us? His love for his children reaches far beyond that of an earthly parent. In fact, his love is so much greater than love between humans that there can be no comparison between the two. He gave his only begotten Son to die on a cruel cross in order that we might return to him. For the person who may refute this idea on the basis that he or she is no longer a child (as depicted in my illustration), remember Jesus's comment in Matthew 18:3–4: "Assuredly, I say unto you, unless you are converted and become as little children, you will by no means enter the kingdom of heaven. Therefore whoever humbles himself as this little child is the greatest in the kingdom of heaven."

I know that this may be a difficult pill to swallow for some, especially in this day when being macho is the "in" thing. If our battle were limited to human beings and what we can see, hear, and touch, then macho would certainly be appropriate. However, because "We do not wrestle against flesh and blood, but against principalities, against powers, against the rulers of the darkness of this age, against spiritual hosts of wickedness in the heavenly places," according to Ephesians 6:12, then it would be to our advantage to humble ourselves and allow the Lord to fight our battles. If we could visualize, even for a moment, all that is arrayed against us in the spiritual world, we would, as little children, hang on to our Lord and refuse to let him go.

In an effort to determine the magnitude of our heavenly Father's love for us, we might take a good, long look at the cross. Just maybe, the way of the cross does lead home to our heavenly Father's heart. Let us take this way of the cross and see where it leads. Paul said, "For the message of the cross is foolishness to those who are perishing, but to us who are being saved it is the power of God" (1 Corinthians 1:18). Again, in Galatians 6:14, he said, "But God forbid that I should boast except in the cross of our Lord Jesus Christ, by whom the whole world has been crucified to me, and I to the world." Paul is saying that the cross upon which the precious blood of Jesus was shed provided the power by which Paul disassociated himself from the world. It is the power of God that empowers us to walk in the Spirit. Without Jesus's shed blood, there would have been no remission of sin (Hebrews 9:22), and therefore the Holy Spirit could never have made our bodies his temple (1 Corinthians 3:16; Romans 8:9). It is through the cross and the shedding of the blood of the Lamb that we are saved, that we are reconciled to the Father, and that we have the Holy Spirit within us. Those who believe in the blood of Jesus for eternal salvation can readily agree with Paul that the cross is the means by which this became possible. In addition, Paul speaks of that same cross as the means by which the world was crucified to him and himself to the world.

It is the power of the cross that makes eternal life possible, allowing us to walk in the Spirit. It further provides deeper intimacy with the Father as we are crucified to the world. There are six references in the Gospels that contain Christ's words concerning the crucifixion of the believer. In Matthew 16:24, we read, "If anyone desires to come after me, let him deny himself, and take up his cross, and follow me." Matthew 10:38, Mark 8:34, Mark 10:21, Luke 9:23, and Luke 14:27 all contain the same theme, and all proceeded from the mouth of the Lord Jesus Christ. It is obvious that Jesus wanted his disciples to take up their individual crosses and follow him. Before pursuing this theme any further, let us be sure that we understand that he is not suggesting that we should be crucified on a physical cross. This obviously cannot be so, for he promised that his yoke would be easy and his burden would be light (Matthew 11:30). No! Only he would bear the burden of Golgotha, but there is a cross that each believer must bear if he or she would be his follower. It is that cross of which Paul speaks in Galatians 6:14, the one that crucifies the carnal self and allows the spirit within each believer to be resurrected unto eternal life. Though we do not suffer the agonies of a physical cross, our cross is patterned after that cross upon which Jesus died. This will be developed in more detail later, but for now, let us continue with the cross of Jesus.

Years ago, I read an article in a magazine that made such an impression on me that I continue to recall it some fifty years later. I do not recall the author's name or the name of the magazine, but the impression, which I received from a single picture in that article, I will never forget. The photograph simply depicted an average church with a sign on the front lawn. The message on that sign read "Send your children to our church, where they will not be frightened by the blood of the cross." I asked myself then, as I do to this day, how can a Christian church teach New Testament Christianity without the shedding of the blood of Jesus Christ?

Paul later says in his letter to the Colossians, "For it pleased the Father that in him [Jesus] all the fullness should dwell, and by him to reconcile all things to himself [the Father], by him, whether things on earth or things in heaven, having made peace through *the blood of the cross.*" (Colossians 1:19–20, emphasis mine).

As we seek to find the way in which the cross leads us home, it might be to our advantage to study further the importance that

God has placed upon the cross. As it pertains to the reconciliation between humankind and God, it appears to be the foundation upon which all else is based. We know that masterfully woven among Old Testament Scriptures, there are prophecies and prophetic events that called for a crucifixion for their fulfillment. Long before the cross as a means of execution was even in existence, these Scriptures told that the Messiah would die in such a way that only the cross could have made it possible.

History tells us that the cross was used first by the Persians in approximately 500 BC. The Romans adopted the slow, agonizing death on the cross as a means of executing their vilest criminals, while lesser offenders were put to death by hanging, decapitation, and other less torturous methods.

Many Old Testament prophecies that predicted the cross date back hundreds of years prior to the Persian Empire. Long before the cross was in use, God had seared it into the prophetic scriptural record. We can also see his hand in detailed events that foretold the crucifixion, from the first sacrifice of helpless animals whose skins were used to cover the nakedness of Adam and Eve (Genesis 3:21) to the sacrifice of his Son at Golgotha. Abel brought a lamb to be sacrificed as an offering unto the Lord, and Genesis 4:4 tells us that God " respected Abel and his offering." At Mount Moriah, Abraham was supposed to sacrifice his only son, Isaac, even as God would sacrifice his only Son at Mount Calvary. Isaac, who fulfilled the symbolic role as a type of Christ, obediently carried the wood for the sacrifice up Moriah, even as Jesus carried the wooden cross up Golgotha. In the end, Isaac was spared, as God provided a ram in his place for the sacrifice, much as he provided Jesus, the Lamb of God, sparing us from death (Genesis 22:1–14).

Realizing that we are bypassing many prophetic events that relate to the Messiah, fast-forward to the time of Moses. Certainly, no foreshadowing circumstance foretells Christ's sacrifice better than Passover. Picture it: Moses has been sent by God from the wilderness back to Egypt to be used by God to free the children of

Israel from four hundred years of Egyptian bondage. Pharaoh has stubbornly refused to allow the Israelites to leave, having held out through nine devastating plagues that God brought upon his land. The tenth plague is recorded in Exodus.

Now the Lord spoke to Moses and Aaron in the land of Egypt, saying, this month shall be your beginning of months; it shall be the first month of the year to you. Speak to all the congregation of Israel, saying: on the 10th of this month every man shall take for himself a Lamb, according to the house of his father, a Lamb for a household. And if the household is too small for the Lamb, let him and his neighbor next to his house take it according to the number of the persons; according to each man's need you shall make your count for the Lamb. Your Lamb shall be without blemish, a male of the first year. You may take it from the sheep or from the goats. Now you shall keep it until the fourteenth day of the same month. Then the whole assembly of the congregation of Israel shall kill it at twilight. And they shall take some of the blood and put it on the two doorposts and on the lentil of the houses where they eat it. Then they shall eat the flesh on that night; roasted in fire, with unleavened bread and with bitter herbs they shall eat it. Do not eat it raw, nor boiled at all with water, but roasted in fire—it's head with its legs and its entrails. You shall let none of it remain until morning, and what remains of it until morning you shall burn with fire. And thus shall you eat it: with a belt on your waist, your sandals on your feet, and your staff in your hand. So you shall eat it in haste. It is the Lord's Passover. For I will pass through the land of Egypt

13

on that night, and will strike all the firstborn in the
land of Egypt, both man and beast; and against all
the gods of Egypt I will execute judgment: I am
the Lord. Now the blood shall be a sign for you
on the houses where you are. And *when I see the
blood, I will pass over you*; and the plague shall not
be on you to destroy you when I strike the land of
Egypt. So this day shall be to you a memorial; and
you shall keep it as a feast to the Lord throughout
your generations. You shall keep it as a feast by an
everlasting ordinance. (Exodus 12:1–14, emphasis
mine)

Before we move on with the present subject, let it be emphasized
that the blood was the protective factor that prevented the death
of anyone inside the building upon which it was placed. The vilest
sinner, residing inside by faith in the protective power of the blood,
was protected from the death angel. This emphasizes the power that
God would place in the blood of the coming Messiah, the eternal
Passover Lamb. For whosoever will believe that the blood of Jesus
was shed for the remission of sin and will, therefore, by faith place
his blood upon the doorpost of his or her heart will be saved from
death into newness of life.

After the Passover lamb had been slain and its blood placed
on the doorposts and lentil, the curse of the tenth plague fell hard
upon the land of Egypt. The firstborn of all the land were slain,
and finally, Pharaoh's heart was softened, and he decided to allow
the children of Israel to leave Egypt. Of course, he later changed his
mind and pursued the freed slaves to the Red Sea, where he and his
army were destroyed by the hand of God.

We cannot fail to see the similarity between the Passover, where
faith in the blood of the unblemished Lamb saved the Israelites from
death, and faith in the blood of the perfect Lamb of God (Jesus)
saves the believer from death. It is even more difficult to ignore the

fact that Jesus's crucifixion fell exactly on Passover. As the traditional Passover was observed in the temple site inside Jerusalem, God's Passover was occurring on Golgotha, just outside the wall of the city. As the Passover lamb was being prepared by the chief priests of Israel, the true Lamb of God was being staked out on a Roman altar—the cross. As the unblemished lamb of the chief priest shed its blood for the sins of Israel for one year, the perfect Lamb of God was shedding his blood for the sins of all humankind for all eternity.

Remember that when the Lord partook of his Last Supper with his disciples, he held up the cup and said, "Drink from it, all of you. For this is My blood of the new covenant, which is shed for many for the remission of sins" (Matthew 26:27–28). This took place at the Passover meal that had been memorialized annually for approximately 1,500 years. The next day, Jesus, who had made that statement, would become the sacrificial Lamb of God.

After the children of Israel were freed from the slavery of Egypt, they wandered in the wilderness for forty years. On one particular leg of their journey from Mount Hor to Edom, they began to complain about the food that God had provided for their sustenance. As a result, fiery serpents were released among them, and many died. The people approached Moses for a solution to the dilemma, and Moses, of course, sought God concerning the matter. In light of the crucifixion, which was to occur over one thousand years later, God's response is plainly clear, but to the children of Israel, it had to appear strange. God's reaction is recorded in Numbers 21:8. "Make a fiery serpent, and set it upon a pole; and it shall be that everyone who is bitten, when he looks at it, shall live." Moses followed God's instructions, and we are told in Numbers 21:9 that every person lived who looked upon the serpent. When we look at this episode in the lives of the children of Israel from the vantage point of the cross of Christ, we can see the obvious prophetic significance, especially in view of the way in which Jesus tied the event to his cross. In John 3:14–15, he said, "And as Moses lifted up the serpent in the wilderness, even so must the Son of man be lifted up, that whosoever believes in Him should not perish but have eternal life." Just as the children of Israel looked upon the snake, which had been placed upon a pole, and were spared from death, so will those who, in faith, look upon Jesus also be spared from death.

Much is prophesied of Jesus's birth, his ministry, and his crucifixion. I have chosen only a few. Let us look at Psalm 22, which contains many references that could have referred only to death by crucifixion. Psalm 22:16 reads, "They pierced My hands and My feet." No other means of execution has ever required the piercing of both hands and feet. What makes this so interesting is that this statement was written approximately one thousand years before Jesus's death and nearly five hundred years before the Persians first used crucifixion as a means of execution. This same Psalm includes at least five other references to our Lord's crucifixion; among them is the mention of men gambling for his garment, a prophecy that was fulfilled in Matthew 27:35, where we are told that the Roman soldiers cast lots for Jesus's garments.

Isaiah 53:4–7 reads:

> Surely He has born our griefs and carried our sorrows; yet we did esteem Him stricken, smitten by God, and afflicted. But He was wounded for our transgressions, He was bruised for our iniquities; the chastisement for our peace was upon Him, and by His stripes we are healed. All we like sheep have gone astray; we have turned, every one, to his own way; and the Lord has laid on Him the iniquity of us all. He was oppressed and He was afflicted, yet He opened not his mouth; He was led as a Lamb to the slaughter, and as a sheep before its shearers is silent, so He opened not His mouth.

Intricately woven into the tapestry of Jewish history are many events that forecast the coming Messiah. Jewish prophets told of his birth, his forthcoming accomplishments, and his death. Micah 5:2 tells us that he would be born in Bethlehem. "But you, Bethlehem Ephratah, though you are little among the thousands of Judah, yet out of you shall come forth to Me the One to be ruler in Israel, whose goings forth are from of old, from everlasting."

Concerning his ministry, we are told in Luke 4:16–21 that immediately after his temptation in the wilderness, Jesus opened his ministry in Nazareth, where he had been brought up. In the synagogue of that city, his work on this earth began with the reading of a prophecy. From Isaiah 61:1–2, he read:

> The Spirit of the Lord God is upon Me, because the Lord has anointed Me to preach good tidings to the poor; He has sent Me to heal the brokenhearted, to proclaim liberty to the captives, and the opening of the prison to those who are bound; to proclaim the acceptable year of the Lord, and the day of vengeance of our God; to comfort all who mourn, to console those who mourn in Zion, to give them beauty for ashes, the oil of joy for mourning, the garment of praise for the spirit of heaviness; that they may be called trees of righteousness, the planting of the Lord, that He may be glorified.

Luke 4:21 makes it patently clear that Jesus is the fulfillment of that prophecy. Having read the Isaiah 61 Scripture, the Bible tells us that Jesus stated, "Today this Scripture is fulfilled in your hearing."

While it is true that many prophecies detailed his birth and ministry, the emphasis in Scripture is placed upon his death, which sealed the new covenant between God and humankind. It is impossible to come away from a study of Scripture without a concrete impression that God intended for his Word to contain the magnitude of his esteem for his Son and what he would accomplish on the cross.

Throughout the Scriptures and with awe- inspiring precision, he detailed what Jesus's coming would mean for humankind.

As we approach the cross, can we expect any less detail in the presentation of the death of his precious Son? No! We should be prepared to search out and embrace the blessing couched within the details. Here, in the death of his Son, we may be able to glimpse the very heart of God. As he watched the events of the cross unfold before him on that dreadful day, we can only imagine the heartbreak that our Father experienced. What mighty force could have prevented the destruction of all humankind in retaliation for the atrocities that his Son was forced to endure? Only his magnificent heart, which is full of love for humankind, could have done so. Since he had choreographed history in order to bring the world to Golgotha, we can be assured that his hand directed the events of the cross, down to the minutest detail. Let us humbly approach the cross, desirous of Holy Spirit revelation as we survey the most wondrous event in history. May we never forget that our Father is not limited to time and space as we are. He knows no yesterday, today, and tomorrow; therefore, it would seem that the agony of the cross is continuously before him.

In the upper room on the night before the crucifixion, Jesus broke the bread, saying, "Take, eat; this is my body" (Matthew 26:26). Jesus's prophecy foretold the breaking of his body, which he would suffer, beginning at Gethsemane and ending when the Roman spear penetrated his side. From each portal, created by each breaking of his body, would flow the redeeming blood necessary for the salvation of humankind.

Jesus became the final Passover Lamb; John the Baptist spoke of him as "The Lamb of God, which takes away the sin of the world" (John 1:29). No fewer than twenty-seven times in the book of Revelation alone, Jesus is called the Lamb of God. Sinful humankind cannot view Jesus apart from his status as the sacrificial Lamb. We, as believers, see him now as the Son of God, in all of his glory as an equal member of the Holy Trinity, but we must approach that esteemed position through his likeness as the Lamb of God.

While it is true that he came to earth as the sacrificial Lamb, it is also true that he bore far more suffering than those lambs previously sacrificed by the Jewish priests. The Passover lambs were slain with a knife to the throat, death resulting quickly from a single wound. However, in Jesus's case, though the end result was the same, his suffering was intensified immeasurably. No Passover lamb experienced hematidrosis due to emotional agony. Neither was a Passover lamb beaten to the point of death. Never was a Passover lamb forced to wear a crown of thorns, nor was a lamb hung by nails from a wooden cross. It was never necessary to pierce the Passover lamb in the side as a proof of death.

It seems that if death due to shedding of blood was all that was necessary for the remission of sin, then God could have arranged to have Jesus die a significantly less horrendous death. Yet the divine timetable placed Jesus on earth precisely at the same time that crucifixion was in use as a means of execution.

It is my intention, God willing, to explore these wounds— fountains, if you will—from which Jesus's precious blood flowed from his body. This, I believe, will help to shed light on the cross, which we, as believers, have been instructed to take up in our effort to follow Christ. May we then find the means by which we may see the carnal self placed on the altar of sacrifice, thus allowing our reborn spirit to obtain control. Through a study of the wounds that he suffered, we may, in addition, gain a greater appreciation for the armor and weaponry that has been placed at the disposal of the new spirit man. Beginning with the loss of blood suffered by Jesus in Gethsemane and proceeding to that which flowed from the wound in his side as he hung on the cross, seven portals were created:

1. Sweat mixed with blood—Gethsemane
2. The Roman scourging
3. The crown of thorns

4. The nail in his right hand
5. The nail in his left hand
6. The nail in his feet
7. The spear in his side

At his Last Supper, Jesus broke the bread and gave a piece to each disciple, telling him to eat it. This seems to suggest that Jesus was admonishing his disciples—and all believers who would follow—to view solemnly and place great importance upon his broken body. While faith in the blood of Jesus, which was shed for the remission of sin and recognized by the wine of the Eucharist, is essential to salvation and eternal life, is there something to be gleaned from a study of his broken body? Is there blessed fundamental truth to be found in the appalling trauma listed above? For Jesus, as has been noted, would have shed his blood and died from a single wound to a carotid artery, just as surely as he did by crucifixion. Surely, there must be spiritual manna that our heavenly Father would have us harvest from the vicious way in which his Son was treated—spiritual food meant to draw us to him.

May the Holy Spirit guide our thinking as we humbly approach the cross in an attempt to survey the broken body of Jesus.

Father, in Jesus's name, lead us through your Holy Spirit to discern all that you would have us know concerning the atrocities that your precious Son was forced to endure in order to secure our salvation. In Jesus's name we ask this. Amen.

TWO GARDENS

So he drove out the man and he placed at
the east of the garden of Eden Cherubims,
and a flaming sword which turned every
way to keep the way of the tree of life.

—Genesis 3:24

Since Adam partook of the forbidden fruit, humankind has longed for a return to God. Humankind was created to have fellowship with God, to love and to be loved by him, and nothing else can satisfy the need for his love. When we are not in fellowship with him, a void is created that demands to be filled.

The love, which was present in the Garden of Eden where our forebears left him, lures the weary soul, much as the North Pole attracts the hand of a magnet. We have taken the handouts offered by this world in which we live, only to find that they do not satisfy our deprived souls. Even Solomon, who is supposed to be the wisest man who ever lived, said, "I have seen all the works that are done under the sun; and, indeed, all is vanity and grasping for the wind" (Ecclesiastes 1:14). This statement came from a man who had everything. Solomon, this wisest of men, was also the richest man who ever lived. "Vanity of vanities says the preacher, vanity of vanities; all is vanity. What profit has a man of all his labor which he toils under the sun?" (Ecclesiastes 1:2–3). However, King David, the father of Solomon, had experienced another dimension, for he had found that relationship with God that transcends the vanities of this world—that haven that makes life worth living.

Only under the umbrella of God's love will we ever find that which is not vanity, for it is in the warm glow of his loving presence that the heart finds that satisfaction that makes life worth living. David certainly knew how to satisfy that longing for God that resulted from the fall of Adam. He simply made God his Shepherd, and having done so, he knew that complete satisfaction that a relationship with God makes possible. In Psalm 23:1, he says, "The Lord is my Shepherd, I shall not want." The longing for that thing that would bring peace and joy to the soul would never be found in the pleasures of this earth, and David knew it. The search was over, and David was content in his relationship with his Lord. We must come to the point where we can say, with David, that we need none of the superficial and temporary pleasures of this earth that are outside the limits of that which our Shepherd has provided.

Adam and Eve were created for fellowship with God; their sole purpose was to be loved by God and to reciprocate by loving him. The ability to give and receive love was as much of an endowment from their Creator as were the physical organs that allowed them natural life. Having lost the capability of accessing divine love by partaking of the forbidden fruit, they died spiritually, just as surely as they would have died physically with the shutdown of the cardiovascular system. While the physiological processes continued to maintain physical life, the separation from the love of God resulted in spiritual death. Whatever Adam and Eve may have appropriated from God, love was the reason—the foundation—for their very existence.

Within this divinely inspired and blessed relationship with the Almighty, there was no spiritual, psychological, or physical need that was not abundantly satisfied. However, Adam and Eve ate the fruit of the forbidden tree, which had been placed by God in the center of the garden of Eden. They were given freedom to eat of any tree, including either of the two trees located in the center of Eden—the Tree of Life and the Tree of Knowledge of Good and Evil (the tree that would bring them death).

When confronted with the Tree of Life and the tree of death, they chose death. In doing so, they initiated a cascade of events that would ultimately lead to their expulsion from the garden of Eden.

Losing all the benefits associated with Eden must have been devastating to the wayward couple. But far and away, the greater loss was the cessation of their intimate relationship with God. They probably did not foresee the physical death that awaited them. In fact, they could have had no concept of what death meant, as they had never experienced it. But we can be assured that they comprehended fully the meaning of spiritual death, even as they walked out of the garden. Adam and Eve had become the first human beings to experience life without the presence of God. The cold, hard fact of life without meaning must have perplexed and confounded them, even as they walked through the gates of Eden. How many times they must have returned, only to find the way barred. They had missed their opportunity to take from the Tree of Life. How long did it take the reality to set in that they would never again walk hand in hand with God while living on the face of this earth? They would never be able to reverse this thing that they brought upon themselves. They had forfeited their right to life. "So He drove out the man; and He placed Cherubim at the East of the Garden of Eden, and a flaming sword which turned every way, to guard the way to the tree of life" (Genesis 3:24). In addition to losing the garden and all of its benefits, Adam and Eve were to live under the sentence of death. As it turned out, this condemnation was not limited to the first couple but also to their progeny. Because of Adam's disobedience, the Tree of Life would be sealed away. No human would ever be able to partake of its fruit.

Although the Creator, at times, intervened in the affairs of humankind, the intimacy of Eden was gone. It was a moment in time fondly remembered and its story passed from generation to generation, but the Tree of Life remained sealed.

After Eden, there were occasionally those special characters from Hebrew history who exhibited, through word and deed, a close affiliation with God. The Creator chose to use them to impact human history, many times in decisive fashion. From the Torah, the Psalms, the prophets, and the historical Scriptures, the benevolent hand of the Creator can be seen.

There were those who walked near to God's heart, but no one could boast of intimacies with God like Adam had experienced before he rejected God's love through his disobedience. Even after the fall, there is evidence of God's love for Adam and Eve. Though little is written of the first couple's response to the dilemma that confronted them, the Scripture does tell us that they "knew their nakedness" (Genesis 3:7). Immediately, they set about trying to hide their shame; they covered their degradation with fig leaves. In God's reaction to their human effort, we see a demonstration of his love and mercy. After his pronouncement of the curses that would come upon Adam and Eve as a result of their disobedience, he made coats from animal skins and clothed them (Genesis 3:21). This was the first of many animal sacrifices that were to come. It was the first prophecy regarding the final plan for the salvation of all humankind. Even before the first family had exited the garden, the Creator began to reveal his master plan for the children of Adam and Eve.

It is hardly coincidental that God would choose another garden to initiate the divine plan to renew free access to the Tree of Life.

To protect the way of the Tree of Life, the angels and the flaming sword had barricaded Eden. Gethsemane, another garden, provided the unveiling of the divine plan for the redemption of humankind— the removal of the obstructing forces, the sword and the angel, and the opening of the door to the reestablishment of complete, unrestricted fellowship with God.

But what or who, after thousands of years, could break the divine seal from the Tree of Life? No individual had ever exhibited the ability to obey God's law. Man had proven to be disobedient by nature, and Adam's disobedience had resulted in the cataclysmic separation between the man and his God.

It was the feast of the Passover in Jerusalem, and Jesus of Nazareth, a young teacher and miracle worker, had arrived in the city with his disciples, presumably to participate in the feast. However, Matthew, one of his disciples, relates that two days prior, Jesus had clearly stated that he would go to Jerusalem to be crucified (Matthew 26:2). Later, at the Passover meal, Jesus drew the attention of his disciples to the bread and wine, referring to them as his body and blood, respectively. He instructed them that they should take the bread and the wine in remembrance of him. After the meal, Jesus led his disciples over the brook, Cedron, to a garden called Gethsemane.

It was there in that place, Gethsemane, in the dark of night, where the Creator revealed to the world his perfect Passover Lamb. The one and only completely obedient man would be sacrificed once and for all for the disobedience of man. "For as by one man's [Adam's] disobedience many were made sinners, so also by one man's [Jesus's] obedience many will be made righteous" (Romans 5:19).

The stage was set for the return of anyone who desired to see and know the truth, the open door through which one could return to the intimate presence of almighty God. This reunion would not be the simple return of the wayfarer to his king. No, those who would choose to return would do so as the children of God. He would be Father to all who would return home through the portal that his Son was about to open.

> Blessed be the God and father of our Lord Jesus Christ, who has blessed us with every spiritual blessing in the heavenly places in Christ: just as he chose us in him before the foundation of the world, that we should be holy and without blame before him in love, having predestinated us to adoption as sons by Jesus Christ to himself, according to the

good pleasure of His will, to the praise of the glory of His grace, by which *He made us accepted in the beloved.* In whom we have redemption through his blood, the forgiveness of sins, according to the riches of his grace … (Ephesians 1:3–6, emphasis mine)

And in Ephesians 1:10, we read, "That in the dispensation of the fullness of times He might gather together in one all things in Christ, both which are in heaven and which are on earth; even in Him." And in Romans 8:15–17, we read, "For you did not receive the spirit of bondage again to fear; but you received the Spirit of adoption, by whom we cry out Abba, Father. The Spirit himself bears witness with our spirit that we are children of God, and if children, then heirs-heirs of God, and joint heirs with Christ, if indeed we suffer with him, that we may also be glorified together." Those who would believe in his Son could now call him Father, Abba, which is Aramaic for Daddy.

Henceforth, the way would be opened, and nothing but the individual's own free will could separate any person from life in the presence of the Father. The one who was and would forever be obedient to God had to present himself as the sacrificial Lamb, for only he, in his perfection, would be worthy to break the seal off the Tree of Life.

Realizing that only he was capable of fulfilling this phenomenal task, Jesus entered the garden to pray. No force in the universe possessed the power to coerce him against his will to walk into the darkness of that garden and the colossal struggle that awaited him there. Only—and I repeat, only—his tender love for each of us held him fast, just as the vines of Mount Moriah held Abraham's ram to be sacrificed in Isaac's place. Jesus was not forced into the agony of Gethsemane; in fact, he did not have to come to this earth. He chose to do so.

However, his willingness to obey the Father in no way diminished the intensity of the struggle that he endured in that garden. The Scripture relates the merciless conflict in Luke 22:44, which reads, "And being in agony, He prayed more earnestly. Then his sweat became like great drops of blood falling down to the ground." Hematidrosis is a condition known to modern medicine. It is caused by extreme anguish and results in the breaking of tiny arterioles in the sweat glands. This, then, results in a blood/sweat mix. It was in agony such as this that Jesus demonstrated the fathomless depths of his love. Couched within his prayer were three pleas to the Father. Three times he cried, "Let this cup pass from me" (Matthew 26:39–44). But the will of his Father would not be altered. The following day, he would experience brutal physical agony—the assumption of the sin and suffering of all humankind and, the most dreadful of all, separation from his Father. He would be consigned to the state of Adam after the fall, when the first man longingly peered back over his shoulder toward the sealed gates of Eden.

All of heaven must have stood by with breathless anticipation as they awaited the final answer from their crown prince. Heavenly hosts must have looked on in awe at the magnanimity of the Almighty's willingness to sacrifice the prince of heaven for the benefit of so completely undeserving humankind.

Incredibly, the world for which this divine drama was enacted slept. The following words, which would change the course of earthly history and fill heaven's Book of Life, went virtually unnoticed by humanity, including his closest disciples, who slept nearby. Jesus said, "Abba, Father, all things are possible for You. Take this cup away from Me; nevertheless not what I will, but what You will" (Mark 14:36). And in Matthew 26:42: "O my father, if this cup may not pass from Me unless I drink it, Your will be done."

His word, spoken in Gethsemane, would begin the process that would break the seal off the Tree of Life, thus providing a way home to all who choose to fellowship with the Father. It was through the blood that was shed in Gethsemane and the following day;

during the events that led to the crucifixion; and of course with the crucifixion itself that Jesus provided not only forgiveness for our sins but for all of our needs. He not only took the sins of the world upon himself, but he also took unto himself all of the turmoil and stress and worry for each of us. By sacrificing his peace, he made peace available for all who would believe. He said, "Peace I leave with you, My peace I give to you; not as the world gives, do I give to you. Let not your heart be troubled, neither let it be afraid" (John 14:27).

Now that we realize the way to the Father lies unobstructed and are aware of God's love, let us seek to know his presence. God challenged Joshua to "Be strong and of good courage" (Joshua 1:6–7, 9), not because of some inherent strength within Joshua but because he, the Almighty, *would be at his side*. Time and time again, the presence of the Father was sufficient to those who knew him, according to the Scripture. David could "Walk through the valley of the shadow of death" without fear, because God was *with him* (Psalm 23). Moses was hesitant to lead the people of God *without the presence of God* (Exodus 33:15). Jeremiah was told by God, "do not be afraid of their faces, *for I am with you to deliver you says the Lord*" (Jeremiah 1:8, emphasis mine). God told the children of Israel, who were under the leadership of King Jehoshaphat, "Fear not, nor be dismayed; tomorrow go against them *for the Lord is with you*" (2 Chronicles 20:17–18, emphasis mine). This was spoken by God at a time when the people were confronted by three hostile armies. The following day, King Jehoshaphat appointed singers to go out in front of the armies and sing praises unto God, and God destroyed the enemies of Judah. In Isaiah 41:10, the children of Israel were told, "*Fear not for I am with you*; be not dismayed for I am your God. I will strengthen you; I will help you; I will uphold you with my righteous right hand" (emphasis mine). In Isaiah 41:13, we read, "*For I, the Lord, your God, will hold your right hand*, saying to you, fear not, I will help you" (emphasis mine).

The greatest obstacle to approaching God will always be that of self-condemnation. Feelings of unworthiness will always be present if we allow them to be. This is true because self- condemnation and a sense of rejection were engraved upon the nature of man after the fall and the resulting eviction from the garden of Eden. That is why it is important that we settle the issue up front. We are unworthy, yes, totally unworthy within ourselves. However, when we have been covered in the blood of Jesus, which is all that the Father requires, we may come to him in perfected holiness. To attempt to approach him in our own holiness is the epitome of self-righteousness, and our righteousness will never satisfy the demands of God. But to ignore what his precious Son has done by shedding his blood at the cross for us is, frankly, incomprehensible, "For He made Him who knew no sin to be sin for us, that we might become the righteousness of God in Him" (2 Corinthians 5:21). So claim your righteousness as the gift that it is. Righteousness, by definition, is right standing with God, meaning that he has made us acceptable to enter into his presence. This special status is achieved by one method and one method only. Through his amazing grace, he gave his only begotten Son, so that whosoever "believed" in him would receive eternal access to the Father. In Romans 4:3, we read, "Abraham believed God and it was accounted to him for righteousness." Jesus, through his obedience, made us righteous and thereby made us accepted in the beloved. Never again will we have to receive condemnation and guilt because we have been, once and for all, delivered through the blood of Jesus. Come boldly to the throne of grace, for if his blood covers you, first-class accommodations await you in the Father's house. Refuse feelings of condemnation and guilt and stand in faith, confessing your righteousness in Christ. If Satan attempts to accuse you, quote 2 Corinthians 5:21 to him or any one of many Scriptures, thus following Jesus's example in the wilderness. He will flee, but if he returns, repeat and repeat again until he determines that you seriously mean to stand on God's Word.

Would that there existed a way to comprehend God's love—to analyze, demonstrate, and describe it. It should be Christianity 101 and a required course, now that his abundant life has been opened

29

to the new believer, especially since we are required to give and to receive love to and from God. However, there is no available instruction manual, and no methodology exists for teaching love. It would be as difficult to explain quantum mechanics to a native living in the jungles of Papua, New Guinea, as it would be to describe the love of the Father to someone else. The songwriter gives a clue as to the overwhelming difficulty by stating that oceans of ink would be necessary in the endeavor. In other words, the human mind will never comprehend the love of God because it is to be spiritually experienced.

Webster's Dictionary defines *love* as "a profoundly tender, passionate *affection* for another person." So, then, we check out the word *affection* and find it defined as "a fond, attachment, devotion, or *love*." This, then, leaves us on the horns of a dilemma—*love* defines *affection*, and *affection* defines *love*. To place an accurate meaning upon the word *love* is impossible, because love is not a mental concept. We may attach mental images or ideas to the word when we hear it, but the truth is that love comes from the heart, and only experience makes it known. Of course, in modern society the term is used to describe acts such as sexual intercourse. It is bantered about in casual conversation, such as, "I love apple pie" or "I love to play golf." These superficial uses of the word only serve to further cloud its meaning.

Most intimate human relationships, such as marriage, began because of this unknown, indescribable entity. People drawn together by this "magnetic force" or "chemistry," which is based on no known rationale, are sometimes bound together throughout their lifetimes.

Anyone who has experienced this human attraction has the ability to understand, to some degree, the meaning of the word *love*, but the experience had to come first. Other relationships can also help to give us some understanding, such as parental love for a child, or vice versa. Our understanding, however, is, at best, a description of the feelings that are engendered by these relationships and the motivations that result from our feelings. Overwhelmed by longing to be together, to hear each other's voices, to touch, or to share, rational thought may be sidelined many times in our efforts to satisfy these desires.

So it is to this love experience that I turn in attempting to describe God's love. Remember how the heart began to sing when that special someone came near. Everything seemed to be filled with new meaning. There was a reason for existence—not to mention that the sky seemed bluer, the grass greener, and all seemed right with the world.

Now, with our rather rudimentary understanding of what is meant by the term *love*, let us return to the One who created the ability to give and receive it. Since *He is love*, according to 1 John 4:16, and he desires to have a loving relationship with every individual on earth, it will never be difficult to find him. If we simply but sincerely open our hearts to him, even with our limited capability, and set our love upon him, he is ever ready to respond. His response is duly recorded: *"Because he has set his love upon Me therefore I will deliver him; I will set him on high because he has known My name. He shall call upon Me and I will answer him; I will be with him in trouble; I will deliver him and honor him. With long life I will satisfy him and show him My salvation"* (Psalm 91:14–16, emphasis mine).

Our Father wants nothing but the best for us, and if we choose to submit our wills to his desire to form a relationship with his children, then we can be assured that he will receive us, and the blessings will be ours.

During the late 1950s and early 1960s, in the middle of the Cold War, I was stationed at Barber's Point Naval Air Station in Hawaii. Our primary mission was to provide an airborne radar barrier for the West Coast, so we flew from Midway Island to the Aleutian Islands. In so doing, our barrier created an extension of the DEW line, which stretched across Canada. Together, this served as a protective umbrella for the North American continent.

We flew every other day for eighteen days, after which we were allowed fourteen days' crew rest back in Hawaii. It was during those two-week intervals in Hawaii that we attended various educational classes. One of those classes left an impression that I shall never forget. I was taken from a well-lighted room and placed into total darkness, in what was referred to as a "night-vision chamber." After being escorted to a chair, I was instructed to focus downward, as though looking from an aircraft downward upon the earth. I was then told to inform the instructor immediately upon seeing anything. I do not remember just how long I sat there in the dark, but some time passed before a faint ray of light began to pierce the darkness. Gradually, the light began to take form and, over a period of time, took on the form of a large city, as it would be expected to appear from an altitude of approximately ten thousand feet. As time passed, airport beacons appeared, and automobile headlights, moving along well-defined thoroughfares, became clearly visible. The impact upon the human eye, when subjected to abrupt changes in lighting, was dramatically emphasized by this experience.

Had we been flying overhead under the conditions experienced upon entry into the chamber, we would have passed, totally unaware of the city's existence. While the military importance of this phenomenon easily can be appreciated, there is another, perhaps more subtle, meaning.

There are most certainly spiritual realities that are vital to a rich, meaningful life. Yet so many times we totally miss them because we fly too high or too fast or simply because we remain in darkness. John 1:4–5 reads, "In Him [Jesus] was life; and the life was the light of men. And the light shines in darkness; and the darkness did not comprehend it." Jesus, again referring to himself as light, said, "Yet a little while is the light with you. Walk while ye have the light, lest darkness come upon you: for he that walketh in darkness knoweth not whither he goeth" (John 12:35 KJV). The light of God is present with us, and he is eager to reveal himself to us. If we will be still and make an attempt to focus upon him, darkness will subside in the glory of his brilliant presence.

God's love, which too often goes unrealized, is most certainly a major necessity for life. We need only to determine to seek his love, and out of the dark shadows of this life, his light will be seen, just as my eyes beheld the light of that city that at first was hidden in darkness.

In summary, God created man and woman and placed them in a garden called Eden, where they proceeded to disobey him. As a result of their disobedience, they were removed from the garden. They lost intimacy with the Creator, and they were banned from ever reentering the garden. They could never again eat of the Tree of Life while on this earth.

Thousands of years later, the process for removing all obstruction to the Tree of Life was initiated by God in another garden called Gethsemane.

Only the obedience of Jesus could open the way to the life-giving tree, and his submission to his Father's will would be revealed to the world the following day at Golgotha. Man could have eaten of the fruit of the beautiful Tree of Life in the garden of Eden, but he chose to eat of the tree that would bring death. Jesus had to eat the fruit of a tree of death (the cross) in order that man could again receive life. The Tree of Life for humankind became a cross.

In the garden of Gethsemane, Jesus made the decision to undergo the horrors of the crucifixion. If we are to return to the benefits of Eden and intimacy with the Father, we must also take up the cross; therefore, the garden of decision looms before us, as it did with Jesus. We are compelled to make the choice, just as he did. Will we be satisfied with Christianity, never knowing a personal relationship with Christ, or will we follow him, bearing our own crosses into that intimacy for which our spirits yearn?

If we opt to follow Christ, we will find, as we take up our crosses, that our burdens are light because he has already borne the load. We are simply carnal creatures, and carnality must be crucified.

However, we cannot crucify our sinful selves any more than we could have placed ourselves upon a Roman cross. It is possible, though unlikely, that we might be able to nail our feet to the cross, but without help, we could never nail a hand to it. It would take one hand to hold the nail and one hand to hold the hammer. So as we make the choice to take up our crosses, we simultaneously make the decision to allow God to complete the crucifixion.

Lord, as we make the decision to take up the cross, wash us clean in the blood that flowed from the body of your Son in the garden of Gethsemane. Help us to realize that the blood of Jesus paved the way for each of us to have the wisdom to see our own crosses and the strength to take them up. May we have the courage, through your Spirit, to enter our Gethsemane and, when there, to say to our crosses, "Your will be done," even as he did. Open our minds to receive all of the wisdom and understanding intrinsic to the following portals (wounds from which the blood of Christ flowed) during the events which surrounded the cross. In Jesus's name, we pray. Amen.

CHAPTER 3

THE CROWN

And when they had platted a crown of thorns
they put it upon his head ...
—Matthew 27:29

Any attempt to return to a relationship with God like that which Adam and Eve experienced in the garden of Eden prior to the fall must begin at the cross. Just as Adam and Eve could have eaten from the Tree of Life, we must receive from our tree of life, the cross. We may never fully comprehend the magnitude of the events that took place at Golgotha, but we must allow the Holy Spirit to reveal the enormity of the price paid by our heavenly Father and his precious Son. It is to the receptive heart that desires to learn of their suffering that God responds. It is through an appreciation for this suffering that we will get a glimpse of God's boundless mercy toward us. As the hymn goes, "On a hill far away stood an old rugged cross, the emblem of suffering and shame ..." Our Father's love for us is revealed in the severity of Jesus's suffering and shame.

Jesus came from his kingdom in heaven to die for this fallen world. His mercy and loving kindness led him to relinquish his royal crown in heaven to become the earthly son of a carpenter. Born in a stable in the little town of Bethlehem and modestly raised in

Nazareth, he shunned the regal life of a heavenly kingdom, humbling himself to become a common man. When tempted by Satan in the wilderness prior to his earthly ministry, he refused to succumb to the offer of earthly kingship. He had completely abandoned his heavenly throne and left his crown in the care of his Father.

Jesus must have recalled that heavenly kingdom and crown during his agony in the garden of Gethsemane. Since he possessed the ability to know the future, he also must have considered the dreaded crown of thorns that would replace his heavenly crown on the following day. Although the crown of thorns, to the human mind, may have represented only a small portion of the horrible suffering that he would endure as the final Passover Lamb, it nevertheless would have been of great significance to his Father. As previously mentioned, nothing that happened to Jesus at his crucifixion was coincidental, and each event associated with the death of his Son was of great consequence to God.

Certainly, for almighty God to allow a group of Roman soldiers to replace Jesus's heavenly diadem with a crown of thorns must have been of supreme importance to the Father. Matthew 27:27–29 reads, "Then the soldiers of the governor took Jesus into the Praetorium and gathered the whole garrison around Him. And they stripped Him and put a scarlet robe on Him. When they had twisted a crown of thorns, they put it on His head, and a reed in His right hand. And they bowed the knee before Him and mocked Him, saying, Hail, King of the Jews!" What additional evidence is necessary to prove, without a doubt, the love and mercy of God? The King of Glory ridiculed and spat upon, the thorns pressed ever deeper into his scalp as the reed struck his head, and the blasphemous cries of the soldiers, "Hail, King of the Jews." The very restraint exhibited by the Father, in view of the shame and degradation that was forced upon his Son, literally cries out from heaven to all humankind, "I love you." It is difficult to comprehend the exorbitant price that had to be paid to reverse the curse of Eden.

Prominent within the curse, which was pronounced in Eden, is the reference to thorns. Genesis 3:17–19 reads:

> Then to Adam He said, because you have heeded the voice of your wife, and have eaten from the tree of which I commanded you, saying, 'you shall not eat of it': cursed is the ground for your sake; in toil you shall eat of it all the days of your life. Both *thorns and thistles it shall bring forth for you*, and you shall eat the herb of the field. In the sweat of your face you shall eat bread till you return to the ground, for out of it you were taken; for dust you are, and to dust you shall return. (emphasis mine)

Adam henceforth would be forced to grow his own food under significant adversity. Only with strenuous effort on his part would the earth yield sustenance for Adam and Eve, in contrast to the bounty they had known. The ability to eat freely from all of Eden's bounty was no more.

One of the greatest prophetic Scriptures in the Bible concerning the coming of Messiah is found in Isaiah 53. In Isaiah 55, the prophet goes on to describe the conditions on earth that result from the Messiah's coming. In Isaiah 55:13, we read, "*Instead of the thorn shall come up the cypress tree*, and instead of the briar shall come up the Myrtle tree; and it shall be to the Lord for a name, for an everlasting sign that shall not be cut off" (emphasis mine). In other words, the prophet is saying that after the Messiah (Jesus) comes, the earth would produce bountifully again for those who would trust in his Son. Jesus's obedience at the cross would reverse the curse that had been placed on the earth by the disobedience of Adam in the garden of Eden. When Adam fell, the resulting curse upon the earth produced thorns. Then Isaiah prophesied, thousands of years later, that the coming of Jesus would signal the removal of the curse, after which the earth would again be productive for those who believed in him.

Jesus bore in his body the curses that had been placed upon humankind through Adam. He gave up the riches of heaven and became poor that we might be freed from the curse of poverty. This clearly is written in 2 Corinthians 8:9, which reads, "For you know the grace of our Lord Jesus Christ, that though He was rich, yet for your sakes He became poor, that you through His poverty might become rich." We can clearly see from this statement that the curse of the thorns was not limited to those who depend directly upon the earth for sustenance (i.e., farmers) but for all humankind. The curse of the thorns was a curse of poverty that would be broken, according to Isaiah, by the coming Messiah. It must be noted here that the reversal of the curse was not limited to monetary gain but touched upon every aspect of life, all of which previously were affected by the curse. The reference to "being made rich" certainly does not mean that we who believe will all become barons of Wall Street. However, it does mean that the individual who believes in the complete work of Jesus on the cross will find heaven waiting to provide every need. Does this then relieve us of all of our responsibilities regarding our own sustenance and that of our families? No! But it does mean that the road to progress on this earth will be far less steep and a great deal smoother. The Holy Spirit within the believer, a fundamental provision made possible by the cross of Christ, assures the availability of abundance in every aspect of life and the wisdom to obtain it.

As the believer accesses the blessed love of the Father, Son, and Holy Spirit, this life, without the curse of poverty, will become more and more a reality.

Let us probe this line of thought a little further by attempting to fully understand what is meant by our new status as children of our Father, the King of heaven. In order to do so, we should return to Romans 8:16–17, which reads, "The Spirit himself bears witness with our spirit that we are children of God, and if children, then heirs—heirs of God and joint heirs with Christ, if indeed we suffer with him, that we may also be glorified together." This observation by the apostle Paul certainly pronounces all believers to be heirs of our Father in heaven. Since he is the King of Kings, and since he is obviously not poverty stricken, and since we, through the cross of Christ and our faith in him, *have been made heirs*, then poverty and lack can have no place in our lives. The curse of poverty, undeniably, has been broken once and for all.

We might go so far as to say that we, as children of God, have been made princes and princesses by the blood of Jesus, since our Father is a King. The Bible tells us that we have been given a crown. Revelation 3:11, Jesus's message to the church in Philadelphia, reads, "Behold, I am coming quickly! Hold fast what you have, that no one may take your crown." The Bible speaks of a crown of rejoicing (1 Thessalonians 2:19), a crown of righteousness (2 Timothy 4:8), a crown of life (James 1:12), a crown of glory (1 Peter 5:4), and again, a crown of life for those who are faithful (Revelation 2:10). All of these Scriptures refer to those who have believed in Jesus and what he did on the cross. The Bible goes even further to say, in Revelation 1:5–6, that we have been made kings and priests. That particular reference reads "Jesus Christ, the faithful witness, the firstborn from the dead, and the *ruler over the Kings of the earth*. To him who loved us and washed us from our sins in his own blood, and *has made us kings and priests* to his God and Father, to him be glory and dominion forever and ever. Amen" (emphasis mine). Jesus sacrificed his heavenly crown and the status for which that crown stood and exchanged it all for an earthly crown of thorns, in order that we might possess a crown of life.

Yes, we have been made kings and priests by the blood of the Lamb, and we have been awarded a crown, but it is incumbent upon us believers to always remember that our crowns are gifts from a loving Lord who paid a dear price for them. Jesus paid the price with his precious blood,which flowed from those hellish thorns as they penetrated deep into his scalp. We must remember to honor him and praise him as we acknowledge that awful payment. One of the best ways in which we can honor him is to show him that we believe in the inerrant truth of his Word, without hesitation or question. His abundance has been made available to us through his shed blood at the cross, but we must appropriate it by faith. We will discuss this in more depth later, but I would like to leave this section with a relevant Scripture. In Joshua 1:8, we read, "this book of the law [the Word of God] shall not depart from your mouth, but you shall meditate in it day and night, that you may observe to do according to all that is written in it. *For then you will make your way prosperous, and then you will have good success*" (emphasis mine).

As we walk in the abundant provision that the cross made available to us, we must give thanks as the Scripture instructs. Ephesians 5:20 reads, "Giving thanks always for all things to God the Father in the name of our Lord Jesus Christ ..." We must always be ready to come before the throne of God, wearing our dearly bought crowns, and always be ready to humbly cast those crowns at the feet of Jesus, even as did the twenty-four elders mentioned in Revelation 4:10. Let us repeat with them their praise, found in Revelation 4:11—"You are worthy, O Lord, to receive glory and honor and power; for You created all things, and by Your will they exist and were created."

When kings ruled the continent of Europe in days of old, they held court surrounded by members of the nobility, who always wore their finest attire in the presence of royalty. Their clothing was made of exquisite materials and bore the rich colors associated with those who were of eminent status. In addition, they embellished their costumes with fine jewelry and gold and silver accessories and usually brandished a family crest. The king's court provided a place where he could entertain foreign dignitaries and meet with heads of state, and due obeisance was expected of all who were present.

It is certainly no less imperative that we, as children of God, enter our Father's court properly attired; in fact, it is impossible to enter while improperly dressed. We cannot enter unless we are washed clean by the blood of Jesus and wearing that which he has graciously provided. We are aware of the crown that he has made available to us; now, let us look into other clothing and equipment with which we have been blessed by the sacrifice of our Lord.

Knights of old also possessed armor, which was appropriate in the presence of the king, during sporting events and times of war. We too have been provided with all the necessary requirements for battle. In Ephesians 6, Paul refers to the military dress necessary for the preparation of God's soldier. As with the crown, all of the armor and equipment mentioned in Ephesians 6 was purchased at the cross by the sacrifice of Jesus. He gave up his life that we might have life, but in order for him to allow himself to be executed, it was necessary for Jesus to surrender all of his protective devices, which would have automatically counteracted any effort to harm him and thereby prevented the crucifixion. In so doing, our Lord made his armor available to all of those who would come to believe in him.

> Finally, my brethren, *be strong in the Lord and in the power of His might. Put on the whole armor of God,* that you may be able to stand against the wiles of the devil. For we do not wrestle against flesh and blood, but against principalities, against powers, against the rulers of the darkness of this age, against spiritual hosts of wickedness in the heavenly places. Therefore *take up the whole armor of God,* that you may be able to withstand in the evil day, and having done all, to stand. Stand therefore, having girded your waist with *truth,* and put on the breastplate of *righteousness,* and having shod your feet with the preparation of the *gospel of peace*; above all, taking the shield of *faith* with which you will be able to quench all the fiery darts of the wicked one. And take the helmet of *salvation* and the sword of the Spirit, which is the *word of God*; praying always

with all prayer and supplication in the Spirit ...
(Ephesians 6:10–18, emphasis mine)

Each piece of the armor described here will be discussed in time, but for now, let us focus on what is referred to as the helmet of salvation. In times of war, kings put away their crowns and led their troops into battle wearing helmets. While we possess a crown with which to approach our Father's throne, much of our time is spent in battle; therefore, we require protection. As a key piece of the soldier's armor, the helmet protects the head and, in turn, the brain, which allows rational thought. Serious injury to this portion of the anatomy obviously renders the soldier useless to himself, his fellow troops, and the army as a whole.

Before we proceed further, let us better understand the need for armor by establishing the scriptural basis for believing that we are in a battle. Peter warned in 1 Peter 5:8, "Be sober, be vigilant; because your adversary the devil walks about like a roaring lion, seeking whom he may devour." This implies that some individuals are vulnerable and capable of being devoured, but those who are sober and vigilant possess the ability to remain immune to Satan's evil designs. In Luke 10:19, Jesus tells his disciples, "Behold, I give you authority to trample on serpents and scorpions [agents of the enemy], and *over all the power of the enemy*, and nothing shall by any means hurt you" (emphasis mine). Although the Bible contains numerous references to the warfare, I believe the Scriptures cited here, along with Paul's admonition in Ephesians 6, are sufficient to substantiate the existence of the battle and the need for vigilance on the part of the believer.

So that we fully appreciate all that has been laid before us, let us now return to the cross. It is obvious that Jesus relinquished his heavenly crown, which represented his exalted status in heaven, and received a man-made crown, which he wore to the cross. By doing so, he provided us with an eternal crown of salvation. Once a person receives Christ as Savior, that individual becomes a child of the heavenly Father. He is "born again" into the family of God, and the crown he has been awarded permanently belongs to him. He is just as secure in his salvation as Noah was when he was in the ark. Just as surely as God shut up Noah inside the ark, God binds the believer for all eternity to his Son. Noah followed God's instructions implicitly in all things pertaining to the ark, which was to be his salvation, and God rewarded Noah's effort. Genesis 7:16 reads, "So those that entered, male and female of all flesh, went in as God had commanded him; *and the Lord shut him in*" (emphasis mine).

The Bible tells us that God also shuts in those in the same way who have believed in Jesus as Lord and Savior. Referring to those believers as sheep, Jesus said, "My sheep hear my voice, and I know them and they follow me. And I give them eternal life, *and they shall never perish; neither shall any one snatch them out of My hand*" (John 10:27–28, emphasis mine). Notice that Jesus said "they shall *never* perish"! This is true security, and it is truly eternal. This is every bit as secure as Noah was in the ark because either state—whether housed in the ark or saved by the blood of Jesus—is sanctioned by God, the Father, and either is held fast by his grace. One word of caution: Satan's attack is very likely to come right here, at the very foundation of Christian life, by causing doubt as to whether we were ever saved in the first place. Herein lies one purpose for wearing our helmets of salvation and the reason why we must have them properly fitted in place. We accomplish this fitting by allowing the Holy Spirit to establish the truth of our salvation at the very outset. This is accomplished by allowing the Lord to express his love toward us on a daily basis. The continuous experience of his love releases us from the need to reconfirm our conversion experience. It is as we walk in his love that we are protected by the helmet of salvation. Once an individual is ensnared by the love of God, he or she becomes less and less conscious of the need for eternal security because in his heart, he knows that he is held firmly and eternally secure in the warmth of divine love. His helmet is firmly in place.

Now we must turn our attention to other methods employed by our adversary. First, we need to remember that our enemy is also our Father's enemy. Since God's primary desire is a loving relationship with his children, Satan's paramount objective is to prevent the establishment of that liaison. Our opponent is quite aware of the fact that when the believer becomes knowledgeable concerning the Father's love and begins to walk in that love, that individual will become less and less vulnerable to his attack. The devil does not mind our activities that are undertaken because of religious obligation instead of response to the love of God. He is keenly aware that such interests have no more power than sounding brass; they may make a lot of noise but seldom produce any lasting positive results (1 Corinthians 13).

The Evil One is highly adept at using circumstances to create doubt concerning God's love for us. From minor frustrations to major crises, he is capable of using these contingencies to create misgiving in our minds concerning our Father's feelings toward us. This wily enemy is readily aware of the fact that he can easily divert our minds to question, "If God really loves me, why did this or that happen to me?" After all, he has been around for our lifetimes, and he has had plenty of time to train us well—many times to unconsciously fulfill his designs. The truth is that God, according to his Word, is always present with the believer; he is always willing to share in any trial that his child might face, and he will provide his "peace that passes understanding" (Philippians 4:7), even in the midst of the most rigorous nightmare. This is the truth! However, our minds, which have been trained by the Enemy to perceive that anything that happens to us is a result of our performance, will interpret a negative situation as punishment for something we have done. We have grown up in a system that requires reward for the good that we have done and punishment for any bad we have done. Therefore, the instant anything happens to us that can be interpreted as punishment, our minds automatically tell us to assume we have done something wrong, and we go off in search of whatever it might have been. It may be that we have done nothing wrong, but our adversary will help us find something that has occurred to explain what we perceive as punishment. He knows that this scenario will always lead to guilt and condemnation, followed by our conclusion that we have been separated from God. The mind, which has been trained for a lifetime under the influence of Satan and his world system, is highly reluctant to receive the truth. This is why, while protected by the helmet of salvation, we must allow the renewal of the mind by the truth found in the Word of God.

When the believer has learned to walk in the love of God prior to the onset of trial or temptation, it is far more likely that he or she will withstand the attack of the Enemy. On the other hand, one who has not daily experienced God's love is less likely to be capable of any appreciable resistance. This is why we must set our minds to receive the love of God and to be established in the fullness of that love. As we train our minds to this end, we will begin to resist the onslaught of Satan because we will come to know that our Lord loves us enough that we can say with Paul, "...all things work together for good to them that love God..." (Romans 8). Our Father wants nothing for us that is not designed for our good. Therefore, when trials come, we can know that they are either initiated by the Devil or designed for our good by our Lord. If they are spawned by the Evil One, we have the power (Luke 10:19) to overcome them. Simply apply to the Father in the name of Jesus to reveal an appropriate Scripture for the occasion, and counter the Enemy by quoting it, in faith, every time he raises his head. You may have to repeat this a few times, but he will inevitably flee. Always remember that he was persistent, even with Jesus in the wilderness. If, however, trial comes from God, you can be assured that it is for your good and will always result in deliverance from something that is holding you back; it will ultimately lead you in a closer walk with the Father. Ask him to reveal the lesson that you are to learn and to provide you with the wisdom to see and understand it. Then request the courage and strength and, above all, his presence to see it through.

It should be obvious that the battle for maintaining a relationship with God occurs within the mind. It is, therefore, necessary that the mind should be protected at all times. Many of us have received salvation unto eternal life, and we are destined to spend eternity with God. However, we may be missing out on some of the benefits of our spiritual helmets, which were provided by the death of our Savior. If we are to experience victory in our lives here on earth, let us seek to know more of this important piece of the armor that has been made available to us. It is an absolute and undeniable truth that our God gave up his precious Son to a bloody death at Golgotha in order to reestablish a loving relationship with each of us. He is no less resolute in his determination to maintain that relationship. For the soul who will determine to apply the Lord's principles to any situation, he will not fail.

When an individual receives Jesus as Savior and Lord, he automatically receives the helmet of salvation, which is the right to live for all eternity in the presence of God, whether on this earth or in the heavenly kingdom. It also serves as protection for the brain, which is the control center of the body and mind, while the mind is being renewed during our lives here on earth. At the instant that an individual becomes a Christian, he or she receives a newborn spirit that is secure in the new state as a member of God's family. Second Corinthians 5:17 reads, "Therefore, if anyone is in Christ, he is a new creation; old things have passed away; behold, all things are become new." However, there is a problem: the mind, which has been developed under the influence of human relationships and a satanically controlled system, must be renewed. This is true because the carnal mind is *enmity against God*. Romans 8:6–7 reads, "For to be carnally minded is death, but to be spiritually minded is life and peace. *Because the carnal mind is enmity against God*; for it is not subject to the law of God, nor indeed can be" (emphasis mine).

It is while wearing our helmets of salvation, God's gift from the cross, that this renewal takes place, giving us complete salvation through the shed blood of Jesus Christ our Lord. According to

Romans 12:2, our minds must be renewed. This Scripture reads, "And do not be conformed to this world, but be transformed by the renewing of your mind, that you may prove what is that good and acceptable and perfect will of God." And in Ephesians 4:23–24, we read, "And be renewed in the spirit of your mind, and that you put on the new man which was created according to God, in true righteousness and holiness." And in his letter to the Colossians, Paul wrote, "Do not lie to one another, since you have put off the old man with his deeds, and have put on the new man who is *renewed in knowledge [mind]* according to the image of him who created him" (Colossians 3:9–10, emphasis mine). The Scripture tells us that "As a person thinketh in his heart, so is he" (Proverbs 23:7 KJV); therefore, it is absolutely necessary for us to take renewal of the mind seriously. If we think that we are defeated, we will remain so until we allow this mental transformation to begin under the guidance of the Holy Spirit. As we do, the mind will come into line with God's Word concerning what we, as his children, should be.

Our spirit (the new man) delights in the hope of arriving in the fullness of God's love. Hence, we are thrilled at the possibilities inherent within Paul's prayer in Ephesians 3:14–19:

> For this reason I bow my knees to the Father of our Lord Jesus Christ, from whom the whole family in heaven and earth is named, that He would grant you, according to the riches of His glory, to be strengthened with might through His Spirit in the inner man, that Christ may dwell in your hearts through faith; that you, being rooted and grounded in love, may be able to comprehend with all the Saints what is the width and length and depth and height—to know the love of Christ which passes knowledge; that you may be filled with all the fullness of God.

In other words, through the love of God, the potential for being filled with the "fullness of God" is set before us, if we will set ourselves to receive it.

How do we set ourselves to receive it? We must first come to the realization that we are, in fact, newborn spirits, but we are also hindered in our quest to walk in the love of God—externally by Satan and internally by a carnal mind that is at enmity with God. *Webster's Dictionary* defines enmity as "a feeling or condition of hostility; hatred; ill will; animosity; antagonism." It is clear that a child of God is up against formidable interference in his attempt to walk in a loving relationship with God, especially when his own mind stands with hostility against his Father. In the light of the foregoing truth, it is easier to understand our inconsistencies in our previous efforts to live the life of peace and joy that is promised in the Scriptures. But let us never lose heart, for it is God's Word that admonishes us to undergo this renewal of the mind and thus gives us hope in the realization that it can be accomplished.

We should begin the renewal of our minds, just as we began our new life in Christ when we first believed in him. We were drawn to this new walk through his grace and by the convicting power of his Holy Spirit, all of which resulted from his great love for us. Certainly, the renewal of our minds will begin right in the middle of his loving presence. To find his love for us, it is necessary to return to that point in history where his love was manifested so clearly. It is there at the cross that we visualize Jesus with the crown of thorns upon his head. Let us remind ourselves that he forfeited his heavenly crown out of pure love for us, and in so doing, he made himself available to receive a man-made crown of thorns. He did not have to do any of this but did so out of his amazing love for us. As a result, we now have a permanent helmet of salvation and a crown of life. May he wash us in the blood that flowed as those thorns pierced his scalp.

Now we must begin the process of mind renewal by focusing on God's *love and his presence within us*. May we set our minds with the resolution of Paul in Romans 8:35–39, determined that nothing shall separate us from the love of God that is in Christ Jesus. Though sickness, poverty, or trial of any kind may come, we will never be separated from the knowledge that Abba loves us.

The Word of God says that for the individual who determines to know God's love and is willing to set this above all else, God will meet him or her at that point of decision.

May we determine to renew our minds to see the Lord as he really is. May we see him as a loving Father who was willing to pay an enormous price in order to have a relationship with his children. May we be renewed to see him in the light of the father of the Prodigal Son, who, having seen his wayward son returning, ran to meet him. Let us see our heavenly Father as analogous to this earthly father referred to in Jesus's parable, who not only ran to meet his son but embraced him with loving care. May we determine to see him as he describes himself in Jeremiah 31:3, which reads, "Yes, I have loved you with everlasting love; therefore with loving kindness I have drawn you." This repetitive referencing of the love of God is intentional because I believe it is impossible to make any progress in our walk with the Lord without first becoming established in his love. I failed in this when I came to know the Lord by allowing myself to become involved in various service-oriented tasks and other "religious" endeavors. These things usurped my time and always left me believing that I was doing the right thing, but I was never able to secure that abundant life that is offered by Christ. Remember, Jude 1:21 says, "*Keep yourselves, in the love of God,* looking for the mercy of our Lord Jesus Christ unto eternal life"(emphasis mine). Let us determine to *keep* ourselves in his love, allowing no activity, religious or otherwise, to interfere.

Just as Satan attempted to establish doubt concerning salvation, he will most certainly attempt to create skepticism where God's love is concerned. Remember that this battle with the adversary is taking place in the carnal mind, which is already at enmity with God. It is here in the mind that he attacks the believer at his or her weakest point. He is very cunning in the use of memories. Through them, he has established strongholds within the mind that, when triggered, can easily destroy wonderful moments of peace and joy in the Lord.

We were born and raised in a system that has been controlled by the Enemy. His forces have influenced every stage of our development. This is the reason why our minds are at enmity with God. He knows our weaknesses, and he attacks us at our weakest point. He takes certain negative events from our past and causes them to become a part of our very makeup. He, therefore, knows exactly what it takes to trigger various emotions, such as anger, pride, or depression. So by placing certain people in our paths or by creating the right circumstances, he can play us like a fiddle. There is no way, even as reborn Christians, that we can withstand the enemy's assault unless our minds are renewed.

Until the mind is renewed, the spirit will be controlled by the mind, which, as we have seen, may be easily controlled by Satan and his system. Our goal should be to harness the mind, therefore bringing it under the control of the Spirit. First Thessalonians 5:23 clearly separates the soul and spirit. It reads, "Now may the God of peace Himself sanctify you completely; and may your whole *spirit, soul, and body* be preserved blameless at the coming of our Lord Jesus Christ"(emphasis mine). And Hebrews 4:12, in referring to the power of God's Word, says, "For the word of God is living and powerful, and sharper than any two-edged sword, piercing even to the division of *soul and spirit* ..."(emphasis mine). As we gain an appreciation for this dichotomy of soul and spirit, we can better understand the war within ourselves. On the one hand, our new spirits, which are influenced by the Holy Spirit, are constantly at odds with our old carnal minds, which are impacted by the Evil One and his world system.

It is by allowing the Holy Spirit to work through our spirits that we begin to gain control of the mind. By so doing, we can short-circuit that which the devil would attempt to accomplish. Simply put, we have the option of what our minds may think concerning any subject. Second Corinthians 10:4–5 reads, "For the weapons of our warfare are not carnal but mighty in God for pulling down strongholds, casting down arguments and every high thing that exalts itself against the knowledge of God, bringing every thought into captivity to the obedience of Christ …"

Some time ago, while reading this particular Scripture, the last phrase of that verse seemed to lift right off the page. It was as though I had never read the phrase before. Prior to that moment, I had always read or quoted the verse as though it referred to my obedience *to* Christ, but it actually reads, "Bringing every thought into captivity to the obedience *of* Christ." It was through Christ's obedience that strongholds would be pulled down, along with anything that would exalt itself against the Word of God, and allow every thought to be brought under control. I would no longer have to struggle with my own thoughts and depend on my own obedience. All of those strongholds created within me could be pulled down if I could but learn to lean upon Christ's obedience.

My thoughts—along with memories, emotions, or anything about my mind that tended to "exalt itself against the knowledge of God"—can be brought under captivity to the obedience *of* Christ. The "knowledge of God" is set forth in the Word of God and proclaims that I am a child of God, I am blessed, I am healed, I am strong, I have peace, I have joy, I am victorious, I am loved, and I am righteous. If my mind, which is at enmity with God, contradicts any of these truths, it must be brought under captivity to the obedience *of* Christ. It was not my obedience but that of Jesus Christ that made the difference. Now, I can take my eyes off my failure to be obedient; in fact, I can remove myself from the picture and focus on Jesus and his obedience. Now, my efforts toward renewal of my mind could be based on what Jesus did (his obedience) and not my behavior, which was strewn with disobedience, much like my previous father, Adam. I could now conceive how bringing every thought into captivity might be possible.

Realizing that Jesus was obedient to the Father in every respect, I wondered if this reference pertaining to his obedience, found in

2 Corinthians, held some specific meaning. So I prayed, asking the Lord to reveal any subtle meanings that it might have for me. Within moments of asking for clarification, the Lord, through his Spirit, quickened the truth in me that although Christ had always been obedient, there was that one time, which underscored the Savior's submissiveness. That time to which the prophets pointed, that time of which the psalmists spoke, that time of which Hebrew historians wrote, that time when Jesus was totally obedient to the Father's will was when he died upon the *cross*. The cross was what I needed to look to for deliverance. It was the blood of Jesus, shed as a result of his obedience to the Father! It was through the cross of Jesus that the power would come for renewal of the mind.

Thoughts may come through the carnal mind, with or without the influence of the Enemy, and may affect us in such a way as to draw us away from fellowship with the Father. However, we have only to confess his love for us and to call those thoughts under captivity to the obedience of Christ. We have the power, because of the obedience of Christ, to allow our spirits to speak. Hence, we can refuse to allow our minds to be affected by anything that would exalt our minds above the knowledge of God (the Word of God), including imaginations (images), emotions (feelings), and thoughts, even dreams. We can refuse memories, and we can keep our minds under control by refusing to think on anything that might stir negative emotions or toxic thoughts. As we repeatedly refuse negative thoughts, imaginations, memories, and emotions, through the power of his obedience, that stronghold of fear or depression will begin to crumble and ultimately will be cast down.

Let us receive the power that was furnished through the blood that flowed from his head as those thorns penetrated his precious scalp. Let us seek to learn of the magnitude of his love, which bade him wear the crown of thorns. He did not have to submit to that shame but chose to wear that man-made crown. Let us stand, determined never to allow our carnal minds to separate us from his blessed love. Let us first allow the truth of the Word of God to birth in us the reality that our minds are enmity against our loving heavenly Father. Then let us begin to speak to our souls (mind, will, emotions—that part of our beings that is separate from the newborn spirit), even as David was prone to do. In Psalm 103:1–5, he says, "Bless the Lord, O my soul; and all that is within me, bless His holy name! Blessed the Lord, oh my soul and forget not all His benefits: who forgives all your iniquities, who heals all your diseases, who redeems your life from destruction, who crowns you with loving kindness and tender mercies, who satisfies your mouth with good things, so that your youth is renewed like the Eagle's."

Let us allow our newborn spirit to assert control by feeding it with the bread of life—Jesus (John 6:51)—and the Word of God. It will surely begin to tame the wayward mind and emotions, bringing them into compatibility with God's Word. When we begin this practice, the Holy Spirit will comfort and guide our spirits by awakening them to the blessed love of the Father. Let us stand, determined never to allow our carnal minds to separate us from his love. Let our minds be renewed so that they are never again a stumbling block, preventing our receiving the abundance of his grace. We want to receive the Spirit that the Father has given to us, the One who was spoken of by Paul in 2 Timothy 1:7, that of "power, and of love, and of a *sound mind*" (emphasis mine).

By taking the helmet, we will begin the process that will lead to death for the old self life. First, we will have established security in Christ for eternity, and second, we will have initiated the process of taking up the cross as we acknowledge that our carnal minds must be renewed in Christ Jesus.

We thank you and praise you, Lord, for wearing a crown of thorns on our behalf and, in so doing, for providing a crown of life and the helmet of salvation for all who believe in you. Lend your assistance, Lord, that we may wear them humbly, and allow him to perform in us that which you intended. Wash us clean in your precious blood, which flowed from your scalp when penetrated by those heinous thorns. In Jesus's name, we ask it. Amen.

CHAPTER 4

THE ROBE

...I have caused thine iniquity to pass from thee,
and I will clothe thee with change of raiment.
—Zechariah 3:4

The same God who, having witnessed the evil world of Noah's day, chose to destroy it then showed mercy when the world determined to brutally murder his own Son. Since Adam, humanity has been credited with little that did not tempt the patience of almighty God. But never before—and certainly not since that day when the Son of God hung upon that cruel cross—has the fate of all humankind hung so precariously in the balance. I cannot imagine any other event in history that could have rivaled the crucifixion in bringing humanity to the brink of destruction. This having been said, it is reasonable to conclude that the love necessary to stay the hand of God from a second destruction of earth is truly beyond human capacity to measure.

What a day that must have been when good and evil stood toe-to-toe in pitched battle over the future of humankind. It is truly ironic that religion, which had prophesied the coming of Messiah to earth, totally missed the significance of this earthshaking event.

To add to the paradox, it is said that the Roman soldiers who participated in this heinous miscarriage of justice gambled for the robe of Jesus Christ, even as he hung on the cross (Matthew 27:35). The King of Glory, the one who held the keys to eternal life for anyone who would simply ask for it, was dying only a few feet away. Surely they had heard the request of the thief who hung on the cross nearby, followed by Jesus's response: "Assuredly, I say to you, today you will be with Me in Paradise" (Luke 23:43). Throughout his ministry, he had offered himself and what he possessed to anyone who chose to respond to him, and other Romans had heard and responded to his message. A Roman centurion had testified that Jesus could save his servant simply by saying the word (Matthew 8:5–13). The good news of his great deeds had been spread abroad throughout Judea and Samaria, and it is reasonable to assume that the soldiers who were involved in the crucifixion of Christ had heard much of this man for whose raiment they gambled. Certainly, they were aware of the fact that this was not the average execution of just another criminal. It is unimaginable that they would not have been shocked to hear a condemned criminal pray for them. In Luke 23:34, we read, "Then Jesus said, 'Father, forgive them, for they do not know what they do.' And they divided his garments and cast lots." It is possible that they may have heard of the woman who had been healed instantaneously of a twelve-year "issue of blood," simply by touching the hem of the garment worn by the one they were executing (Matthew 9:20). Those soldiers had touched the garment as they removed it from the body of Christ, and they certainly examined the robe as they gambled for it. They were in such close proximity to the one who had exhibited such power to save and to heal, even close enough to hear his voice and to touch his clothing, yet the Bible gives no indication that the soldiers possessed even the slightest inkling of the significance of the events that were unfolding in their presence. After Jesus's death, we are told that the Roman centurion "...glorified God saying 'Certainly this was a righteous man' " (Luke 23:47 KJV). Could it be possible that, even now, those

captive to Babylon; two previous deportations of Jewish citizens had taken place, the first dating back to approximately 607 BC when Nebuchadnezzar first took Jerusalem. The Babylonian Empire was subsequently conquered by Cyrus the Great of Medo- Persia who, shortly thereafter, decreed that the Jews could return to Judea, rebuild Jerusalem and the Temple, and reestablish Hebrew worship. No formal worship for the Jewish people had transpired throughout the years of captivity in Babylon.

It was in this setting that Zechariah had his vision of Joshua (the high priest), standing in filthy garments before the angel of the Lord. It is very interesting to note that Satan is also present "to resist Joshua" (Zechariah 3:1). We have to understand that Joshua, along with the remnant of the children of Israel returning from Babylon, had, for years, known only the wrath of God. Because of their disobedience, they had seen the destruction of their temple, along with the city of Jerusalem. They had been carried to Babylon, and for years they had lived under pagan influence. At the time of the prophet Zechariah's vision, they had returned to their homeland; now, they were in the process of returning to the worship of their God.

Clearly, Joshua's filthy raiment speaks of the sin-stained life to which those who had been held captive under the heathen influence of Babylon had been subjected. This is quite typical of the believer's position as he comes to Jesus. Just as the Prodigal came to the father wearing clothing soiled with the mud of his previous life, so Joshua stood before the angel of the Lord in his soiled garments. There was nothing that Joshua could have done to wash away the stains of Babylon, and by the same token, there is nothing we can do within ourselves to remove the filth from our lives. We must come to the realization that the sacrifice of Jesus was and is far more than enough to clothe, in robes of white, anyone who chooses to come to him.

It is of note that Zechariah's prophecy leaps ahead approximately five hundred years into the future, to the time of Messiah's coming. In Zechariah 3:8, he speaks of "my servant the Branch." Further, in Zechariah 3:9, "I will remove the iniquity of that land in one day."

This undoubtedly refers to Jesus as "the Branch," who would remove the iniquity of us all in that one day at Golgotha.

We cannot abandon this moment in history without adding further emphasis to the presence of the Evil One. Too many have believed in Jesus as Lord and received their white robes that have been washed clean in the blood of the Lamb, only to find themselves defeated and unable to stand because of Satan's resistance. You see, as discussed in the previous chapter, he has had thousands of years to perfect his methodology, and he is expert at administering it. At first, his strategy may appear rather complex, but actually, it is quite simple. At the risk of sounding repetitious, Satan always appears as the accuser, and if he can cause us to join in with him in accusing ourselves, he will have won the battle. Just like the Prodigal who saw himself as unworthy to return to the father's house as his son, we too will forfeit our right to fellowship with our Father if we cannot receive the robe that was bought for us by the blood that was shed at Calvary.

As Joshua received his clothing that had been provided by God (he provided nothing for himself), we too must receive that which has been made available to us. Having done this, we must determine to receive no condemnation. When we sin, we must go to the Father immediately, wearing the robe provided for us by Christ, and ask for his forgiveness and his cleansing. Remember that God loves you, and he is not ready to harm or forsake you. You have been washed clean by the blood of Jesus, and God does not condemn you. Satan can only condemn you if you allow it. Refuse his condemnation! Do not allow him to coerce you into any kind of self-righteous works in an attempt to pay for the sin. Jesus has already paid for it. We must put our faith in what Jesus has already done. Romans 5:1 reads, "Therefore, having been justified by *faith*, we have peace with God through our Lord Jesus Christ, through whom also we have access by faith into this grace in which we stand, and rejoice in hope of the glory of God" (emphasis mine).

It is here that we follow Jesus by taking up our own crosses, through faith in his faithfulness to forgive us our sins, and by refusing to attempt to atone for our sins through our own works.

God's love for us is limitless. He is patient with his children and willing to make a way of escape for any sin and to cleanse us from it (1 John 1:9; 1 Corinthians 10:13). Some things that are ingrained in the old carnal nature may take time to eradicate, but if we are faithful in bringing them before him, he is more than faithful enough to cleanse us. I say again, we cannot fall into the old trap of trying to cleanse ourselves because when that happens, we will fail, and when we fail, we will begin again to accuse ourselves and ultimately fall again into a life of self-condemnation. This course of action will always lead to defeat. This is why it is so important that we stay with the scriptural instruction, which is confession and faith in God to cleanse us. If we sin, and we confess, as instructed, and condemnation raises its ugly head, we simply tell the accuser that this sin has been placed under the blood of Jesus, and then we rest in his amazing grace.

We have choices to make; we can choose to be caught up in willful sinning or struggle at attempting to rise above sin through our own efforts, or we can choose that rest that Jesus provides by donning the robe, which he has provided. We put on that robe by choosing to walk in the righteousness of God through faith in Jesus.

In making our choice, let us remember that the chief priests of Israel proceeded with a routine of self-sufficiency and missed the real (God-ordained) meaning behind the Passover feast. Most of the Romans also missed the significance of the events in which they had become involved. They were executing the God of all creation, the very one who was capable of satisfying all the needs of a lifetime and throughout eternity. May we absolutely refuse to be caught up in the trappings of Christianity and miss that loving relationship with our Father, Jesus, and the Holy Spirit.

The Bible teaches us that we will wear a robe someday. Revelation 7:14 speaks of those who came out of great tribulation, having washed their robes, making them white with the blood of the Lamb. Revelation 7:9–10 reads, "After these things I looked, and behold, a great multitude which no one could number, of all nations, tribes, peoples, and tongues, standing before the throne and before the Lamb, clothed with *white robes*, with palm branches in their hands, and crying out with a loud voice, saying, Salvation belongs to our God who sits on the throne, and to the Lamb!" (emphasis mine). Revelation 6:11 speaks of the saints being given robes, and Revelation 19 tells us that the armies that follow Christ to Armageddon will be wearing white, clean garments.

But for now, let us be satisfied with the spiritual robe, which the blood of Christ shed at Calvary provided for us. Just as Joshua the priest was given a white robe to wear for his priestly ministries before the Lord, we too have been made priests, and we too have been given robes of white to wear before the throne of grace. Revelation 1:5–6 reads, "To Him who loved us and washed us from our sins in His own blood, and has made us kings and *priests,* to His God and Father, to Him be glory and dominion forever and ever. Amen" (emphasis mine). And in 1 Peter 2:9, those who believe in Christ are referred to as a "*royal priesthood.*"

Jesus sacrificed his robe so that we might be provided with a robe; now, let us move on to another reason for which Jesus was stripped of his robe.

When Jesus stated that the unleavened bread of the Passover meal symbolized his *broken body*, he must have been thinking about the Roman scourging that he would be forced to endure the following day.

Scourging was a preliminary to all Roman crucifixions. Clothing was removed, and the criminal was bound by his hands to an upright flogging post. According to the *Theological Dictionary of the New Testament* (Kittel, volume IV, page 517), scourging is described as follows: "The prospective crucifixion victim, as a rule, was first subjected to flagellation, i.e. a beating with a three thong whip (fashioned of platted leather, and studded with bone and metal). The victim was stripped naked and then was secured with leather ties. He was then beaten from his upper back to the lower extremities of his legs. The flesh was flayed from the muscle. Eventually muscle could be shredded from the bone. The bones of the back, including the spinal column might well be exposed in a bloody mass. Not infrequently these whippings were fatal."

Commenting on Jesus's scourging in the *Journal of the American Medical Association*, March 21, 1986, Dr. William Edwards notes, "This severe scourging with its intense pain and appreciable blood loss, most probably left Jesus in a pre-shock state. Moreover hematidrosis had rendered his skin particularly tender. The physical and mental abuse meted out by the Jews and the Romans, as well as the lack of food, water, and sleep, also contributed to his generally weakened state. Therefore, even before the actual crucifixion, Jesus' physical condition was at least serious and possibly critical. The actual cause of death was the loss of blood volume and the inability to breathe due to the extension of the body."

Just prior to the onset of blessed, anesthesia-producing hypovolemic shock (that state that follows massive loss of body fluids), the victim was cut down from the whipping post and taken to the place of crucifixion. However, in the case of Jesus's crucifixion, the Scripture tells us that Jesus was crowned with thorns, beaten with a stick, and spat upon, in addition to the horrors of scourging (Mark 15:19). All of the information I have gathered appears to indicate that the victim actually suffocated when the body was so weakened that it prevented him from taking the weight off his arms by pushing up with his legs. This is the reason why the Romans, in order to expedite the execution, would break the legs of the victim. Most died within twenty-four to thirty-six hours, but the priests prevailed upon Pilate to expedite this crucifixion because the following day was a holy day. The legs of the two thieves were broken, but Jesus's legs were spared when it was found that he had already ceased to live.

It is without question that Jesus suffered horribly, from the time spent in Gethsemane through the pre-crucifixion events and, of course, the crucifixion itself. But the scourging he was forced to endure arguably was the most horrific of all the tortures he received. This was the point at which his body was seriously broken, a painful ordeal that could have possibly resulted in death prior to the crucifixion. It certainly went far toward fulfilling Isaiah's prophecy.

> He has no form or comeliness; and when we see Him, there is no beauty that we should desire Him. He is despised and rejected by men, a Man of sorrows and acquainted with grief. And we hid, as it were, our faces from Him; He was despised, and we did not esteem Him. Surely He has born our griefs and carried our sorrows; yet we esteem Him stricken, smitten by God, and afflicted. But He was wounded for our transgressions, He was bruised for our iniquities; the chastisement for our peace was upon Him, *and by His stripes we are healed.* (Isaiah 53:2–5, emphasis mine)

Isaiah's prophecy heralded the scourging of Jesus, hundreds of years before the Roman Empire came into being. God was not taken by surprise at the horrible treatment his son received. In fact, in Isaiah 53:10, we read, "Yet it pleased the Lord to bruise Him; He has put Him to grief. When You make His soul an offering for sin, He shall see His seed, He shall prolong His days..." And in Isaiah 53:11, "He shall see the labor of His soul, and be satisfied. By His knowledge My righteous Servant shall justify many, for He shall bear their iniquities." And last, in Isaiah 53:12, "Therefore I will divide Him a portion with the great, and He shall divide the spoil with the strong, because He poured out His soul unto death, and He was numbered with the transgressors, and He bore the sin of many, and made intercession for the transgressors."

This messianic prophecy in Isaiah, written hundreds of years before Jesus went to the cross, leaves little doubt that Jesus would be severely beaten and that his stripes would result in healing for the believer. Even a cursory reading of the four Gospels clearly reveals that prior to the cross, a large portion of Jesus's earthly ministry consisted of healing. Those who came to him requesting healing were never turned away. He seemed to enjoy seeing the lame walk, the leper made clean, deaf ears made to hear, and blind eyes made to see.

But before proceeding further into a discussion of healing, we should consider a basic question: is it God's will for every person to be healed? Personally, I believe there is no scriptural basis for believing otherwise. But let me set the record straight; though I have reached the age of seventy-six, I have not always been without illness, which, at times, has been very serious. I have experienced a myocardial infarction (heart attack) and have undergone cardiac surgery on two separate occasions. I am also a thirteen-year cancer survivor. My first wife died in 1997 of complications related to diabetes, and my present wife is a three-year survivor of breast cancer. So, then, one might ask, "What makes you believe in divine healing?" And that would be a reasonable question in light of the above, but the answer is fairly simple. I believe that the Bible is the inspired Word of almighty God. I believe that God makes no mistakes and that every word he has spoken into the Scriptures is error-free. Hence, when his Word says that we are healed by the stripes of his dear Son, I believe that we are healed by the stripes of his dear Son. (We will discuss the truth of God's Word in more detail later.) For now, let me say that I have not always been quite so firm as to the truth of God's Word, especially in the area of healing. My training as a physician caused me to place more reliance on myself and my profession than I should have, though I see no discrepancy between faith and science. At this point—somewhat older and maybe a little wiser—I have come to believe that faith in God is the primary healing agent, whether he chooses to use medicine or the "miraculous" to achieve the ultimate end. I believe that in giving humankind the blessed gift of modern medicine, God proved that he wanted man to walk in health.

God certainly created Adam without sickness or disease, and only after the fall did illness come upon man as part of the curse of death. The human body's God-given intrinsic ability to heal itself serves as strong evidence of God's desire to see us healthy. The biological and physiological processes that are triggered with a simple laceration to the skin are simply mind-boggling in their complexities, and they are all designed to produce healing. We have come to take this miraculous healing process for granted, having witnessed it so many times throughout our lives, and only when it fails to work do we become alarmed enough to acknowledge the existence of this marvelous God-given life-saving mechanism. A casual study of cell regeneration and maintenance leaves little doubt that the body was created by God to maintain itself in a healthy state.

God, through modern medicine, has taught us a great deal about how to assist the body in keeping itself healthy. It has provided us with the knowledge of various proteins, carbohydrates, fats, minerals, and vitamins and how they help to maintain a healthy state. Modern medicine has also made available various medical and surgical procedures with which to prolong life. Infectious diseases that often are eradicated within a few days using antibiotics would have proved fatal only a few years ago. Serious heart disease, which was considered deadly only a few decades ago, can now be corrected within a few hours in a surgical suite. Some lethal diseases have been wiped out, and though some, such as cancer, are still with us, major strides have been made in decreasing the impact upon the individual and society.

In light of the evidence given above and while the Scriptures teach that God wills that his children walk in health, many Christian people are sick. Why is this true? Admittedly, we do not have all the answers; there are many cases for which there seems to be no human explanation. A case that comes to mind is a young boy of approximately seven or eight years old, whom I treated for several years. This young fellow was a treat to know, and I shall never forget the pleasure he brought into my life. On one occasion, his mother brought the child to the office, complaining that he recently had developed double vision. After a thorough evaluation, my initial concerns were verified. This wonderful child had developed an aggressive brain tumor; the prognosis gave him only a few months to live. I prayed for this little guy, and I tried to believe that he might be healed, but it was to no avail. A few months passed, and he died. I realize that my previous education, both academic and experiential, had provided me with knowledge concerning the aggressiveness of the particular cancer and that this may have tainted my faith in a positive outcome for this child. However, many others also were praying for this young man. To this day, I have no explanation of why this otherwise healthy young fellow developed the cancer in the first place or why God would not heal him, but over the years, I have learned to leave it in God's hands. I have to add that I was impressed that during the three or four months that the child lived, he always appeared to be in a state of peace and never revealed any anxiety in my presence.

There have been many other cases in which I experienced the loss of patients and loved ones throughout my lifetime, and while I suffered the loss, I never failed to know the comforting presence of almighty God. Especially with the loss of my first wife, I experienced serious mourning and sadness over the separation, but I knew his presence, and that allowed me to work through the grief. Many cases seemingly had no explanation of why prayers for healing were not answered in the affirmative, inevitably leaving disappointment and grief in their wake. Someday maybe we will understand, but for now, we must be content with leaving those questions in the hands of the God, who loves us. Let us now look to some cases in which there were answers.

During his ministry on earth, Jesus spent much of his time healing the sick. He was known to have asked the man with a thirty-eight–year infirmity, "Do you want to be healed?" This occurred at the pool of Bethesda, where many were gathered, presumably with hope of being healed. Yet Jesus asked the man, "Do you want to be made well?" (John 5:6). Clearly, there was some question as to the man's desire to be healed. Some say that they want to be made whole, but in truth, they have come to enjoy the attention and other benefits that infirmity can afford them. This man, spoken of in John 5, received his healing when he responded in the affirmative to the question posed by Jesus. However, there probably are those for whom no amount of prayer will ever result in healing because, in fact, they choose not to be healed.

In John 9:7, we read about Jesus's instruction to the blind man, telling him to go and wash in the pool of Siloam. In this case, the individual responded positively to the instruction and was healed of blindness. There are those, however, who do not hear and obey the instruction. They refuse to confront a bad habit, which could lead to serious illness. They hear the wisdom and guidance of the Spirit, but they do not respond. This is in no way meant to create guilt and condemnation for that one who is having difficulty with an addiction but is an attempt to urge that person to seek the Lord concerning his or her stronghold. This is also for the one who will not accept the reality that the addiction may lead to serious illness and possibly death. There is hope for anyone who will bring the problem to our loving Lord and allow him to cleanse us and break the bonds that enslave.

Then there are those who have no faith for healing. While believing strongly in some areas, such as salvation or finances, and standing firm on the truth of God's Word, they have developed no faith where healing is concerned. Never having been taught the scriptural basis for healing, there is consequently no framework on which to build faith in it. In this case, it is imperative that we begin with the basic realization of God's love for us. As already alluded to, we must start from the affirmation that if he loves us, surely he does not want us to be sick. Consider this: I love my child;

therefore, I do not want my child to be ill. My heavenly Father loves me; therefore, when I look at it rationally, it is reasonable to believe that he doesn't want me to be sick either. From the vantage point of believing in God's love for me and his obvious desire for my health, I can then begin more easily to believe in what he has said in his Word concerning healing.

Mary and Martha, sisters of Lazarus of Bethany, believed that Jesus could heal their sick brother. So they sent messengers to Jesus, requesting that he come and heal Lazarus, but Jesus delayed, and Lazarus died (John 11). After hearing of Lazarus's death, Jesus then went to Bethany, the hometown of Mary and Martha, and there, he raised Lazarus from the dead. To prove his power over the grave and to glorify God, Jesus had delayed the healing of Lazarus. In other words, Jesus had allowed Lazarus to be sick unto death in order to glorify God. If an illness or infirmity somehow magnifies and gives glory to God, there is obvious justification for it. There have been and are today many who give glory to God, even while subjected to the worst of illness or injury. From sickbeds and wheelchairs, many give testimony to those who are hurting throughout the world, thereby giving glory to our Lord and hope to those who suffer in a like manner. Rather than eradicating the illness or infirmity, sometimes the Lord will minister through it to a lost world.

It is painfully obvious that illness exists, both for the believer and nonbeliever alike, and that—for whatever reason—some do not receive healing. But I repeat that I believe that if we, as his children, hear and obey him, that short of some special circumstance, God's master plan is for all of his children to be healed. In Adam's perfect world, there was no sickness and disease; there was no dying process. When Jesus received the scourging prior to his crucifixion and later died at Golgotha, he lifted us above the state in which Adam existed prior to the fall. He prepared the way for our spiritual rebirth, placing within us a new spirit, which will live forever, with or without a natural organic flesh-and-bone body. Though we are taught to respect and to care for our earthly bodies, they are destined to pass, while the spirit lives on throughout eternity. This new spiritual man or woman will, one day, receive a new and eternal body that will be designed to live with our Lord in his heavenly kingdom (2 Corinthians 5:1). Until that day comes, let us become resolute in our determination to walk in the truth of God's Word, receiving the healing that Jesus obtained for us by his stripes. Let us begin to train our minds, which previously were at enmity with God, by bringing them under subjection to the obedience of Christ, where healing is concerned. Let us repeat—over and over again, if need be—with David in Psalm 103:1–5, "Bless the Lord, oh my soul; and all that is within me, bless His holy name! Bless the Lord, oh my soul, and forget not all His benefits: Who forgives all your iniquities, Who *heals all your diseases*, Who redeems your life from destruction, Who crowns you with loving kindness and tender mercies Who satisfies your mouth with good things, so that you're youth is renewed like the Eagle's" (emphasis mine).

In his loving and kind presence, we will find healing for spirit, soul, and body. As we become closer and closer to him, it is here that we realize that he is our healing, just as he is everything to us. He is our righteousness; he is our protector; he is our provider; he is our peace; he is our shepherd and guide; he is the God who is with us; and he is our *healer*. According to Exodus 15:26, "If you diligently heed the voice of the Lord your God and do what is right in His sight, give ear to His commandments and keep all His statutes, I will put none of the diseases on you which I have brought on the Egyptians, *for I am the Lord who heals you*" (emphasis mine). This was, of course, spoken to the children of Israel after they departed from Egypt and were under the Law. We can take heart in the fact that we, by faith in the grace of God, now walk in his Son. Malachi's prophecy concerning Jesus, which is found in Malachi 4:2, reads, "But to you who fear My name *the Sun of Righteousness shall arise with healing in His wings* ..." And Peter, speaking of Jesus, states in 1 Peter 2:24, "...who Himself bore our sins in His own body on the tree, that we, having died to sins, might live for righteousness-- *by whose stripes you were healed"* (emphasis mine).

It is in Jesus that we live and move and have our being. In him, this physical body, just like the carnal mind, becomes secondary to the new spirit. His new and living spirit, which was provided by the Lord at his death for anyone who would believe, cannot help but bring life and healing to the physical body. And if physical healing does not result, the new spirit of life in Christ will shine forth—from the wheelchair or from wherever he places us—to the glory of God.

Yes, prior to his crucifixion, Jesus allowed the Romans to strip him of his robe, and like a lamb to the slaughter, he allowed them to mercilessly beat him. To those who choose to believe, his sacrifice became a healing balm for the spirit, soul, and body. He said to his disciples at their last meal together prior to the cross, that the bread was to be eaten as if it were his body that was broken for them. Of course, this was meant not only for the disciples but for anyone who would believe in him and his sacrifice. Each time we receive communion, we receive the broken bread as a likeness of Jesus's broken body, just as it was sacrificed under the Roman scourging, in order that we might be made whole.

Hebrews 4:16 reads, "Let us therefore come boldly to the throne of grace, that we may obtain mercy and find grace to help in time of need." Yes, come boldly, wearing the robe that Jesus provided and the crown he provided, and we come washed completely clean in his precious blood. It is then that we are in a position to ask of our loving heavenly Father, healing of the mind, will, emotions, and body.

In addition, we are then ready to take up our crosses by surrendering these bodies to the ownership of the Holy Spirit. The spiritual revelation that my body belongs to God and is indwelt by his Holy Spirit relieves me of any responsibility for healing and health, except as the Holy Spirit directs. We can then be assured that God will care for the body, which has been surrendered to his service, for since he created the human organism, he is well

CHAPTER 5

THE SHIELD

But thou, O Lord, art a shield for me; my glory,
and the lifter up of mine head.

—Psalm 3:3

When the brutal scourging was finally completed to the satisfaction
of the centurion in charge of the execution, the condemned criminal
would have been forced to carry his cross or the horizontal crossbeam
to the place of crucifixion. In Jesus's case, having suffered through
hematidrosis, a sleepless night, probable lack of nourishment, and
the hideous Roman scourging, he collapsed under the weight of the
heavy wooden beam.

Simon the Cyrene, a bystander, was called upon to aid Jesus as the
processional made its way down what is today called Via Dolorosa,
through the city gate, and finally to the place of crucifixion. There
upon the hill called Golgotha, Jesus was pinned to the wooden cross
by heavy metal spikes. One spike was used for each of his upper
extremities, and one spike pierced both feet. Some controversy has
existed as to whether the spikes were nailed through the palms
of his hands or through his wrists. However, there seems to be
a consensus—at least in the medical literature—that the tissues

forming the hand would have been inadequate to support the weight of Jesus's body.

Whatever the case may have been, we know that Jesus was fastened to the cross by metal spikes and that he was unable to move either hands or feet. He had willingly sacrificed his freedom in exchange for ours. Surely he had demonstrated, during his brief ministry on earth, his great faith in his heavenly Father. He knew that he could pray the prayer that would have ended his suffering and his death, even at this late stage of the process of his execution. Fortunately for all of us who would later place our confidence in him, he did not pray that prayer. In fact, he quietly sacrificed his faith, which could have called ten thousand angels to deliver him. In so doing, he consented to his death. This then opened the way for the believer to walk in Jesus's faith. One might say that he sacrificed his shield of faith, and in so doing managed to open the way for us to take up his shield of faith.

The faith of Jesus had healed the sick, fed the hungry, quieted the storm, and even raised the dead. As the Son of the Almighty, he possessed an impenetrable shield of faith. No force, including the Roman Empire or Satan himself, could pierce It. Through his faith, he had spoken this world into existence. He spoke the word, and there was light. He spoke the word, and dry land appeared where there had been none before. He spoke the word, and humankind came into existence. Hebrews 11:3 reads, "By faith we understand that the worlds were framed by the word of God, so that the things which are seen were not made of things which are visible." Jesus shared power equally with the Father and the Holy Spirit (Philippians 2:5–6), and in John 1:3KJV, we are told, "All things were made by him[Jesus]; and without him was not anything made that was made".

Having possessed such great faith and power, is it any wonder that Jesus had to remain quiet before Pilate, Herod, and the chief priests? His primary mission in coming to this earth was to die on the cross, as a sacrifice for our sins; therefore, to have given any utterance to the contrary might have thwarted his purpose. The storm was calmed by Jesus's using three words: "peace, be still" (Mark 4:39). Those same words would have quieted the storm that had been created by his adversaries, the Jewish religious hierarchy, the Roman Empire, and Satan himself.

Such faith that calls worlds into existence could have easily been brought to bear by the Son of God, had he opted to do so. Instead, however, he laid down his shield that we might be capable of taking up the challenge posed by Paul in Ephesians 6:16, which admonishes us to take up the shield of faith, above all, that we may quench all the fiery darts of the wicked.

Not only does a strong, vibrant faith quench the fiery darts of our adversaries, but, more importantly, without it we cannot please God. Hebrews 11:6 reads, "But without faith it is impossible to please Him, for he who comes to God must believe that He is, and that He is a rewarder of those who diligently seek Him." Adam and Eve revealed their unbelief or lack of faith in God's Word when they chose to listen to Satan. They were then separated from God as a result of their unbelief. God had said that if they ate of the Tree of Knowledge of Good and Evil, they would die. Satan then called God a liar by telling Adam and Eve that they would not die. Simply put, Adam and Eve, by agreeing with Satan, also called God a liar. In so doing, they told God that they did not believe his Word to be the truth. When we then reveal faith in his Word, our action is diametrically opposed to that of Adam and Eve. Just as their lack of faith caused separation from God, our faith creates reunion with him. Our God, who desires a relationship with his children, is therefore pleased by our faith, and without it, we cannot please him. Jesus laid down his faith, allowing himself to be crucified that we might take up our shield of faith and, by believing his Word, return to our Father. As we approach the fourth portal from which blood flowed from the body of our Lord as he hung upon the cross, let us see the precious blood of Jesus streaming from his hand, which would have borne his shield of faith. Remember, then, that as we take up the shield of faith, we are receiving his shield, for it, along with all of the other armor, belongs to God. We are to *"take up the whole armor of God."* With our new shields, we are able to access the presence of our Father at any time.

It is here in his loving presence that our faith matures. The more we become aware of his great love and his grace, which has been poured out upon us, the more we believe his Word. Conversely, if we are not experiencing his love, it is far more difficult to accept the truth of his words of forgiveness or to receive any of his promises, which all depend upon faith for their fulfillment. The Bible tells us that *faith works by love* (Galatians 5:6). It makes very good sense that good things come to us more readily from those who love us. If I know my earthly father loves me, I have little trouble asking for something that I need. Hence, I certainly believe that there is a high degree of probability that I will receive that for which I have asked. I do not have to study faith books or rely on the testimony of someone else. No, if I know his heart and fully realize his love for me, I simply expect to receive. I have it on good authority (the Bible) that this is exactly how our heavenly Father wishes us to approach his throne. He does not want us to come haltingly but with a boldness borne out of love and respect, as children of a loving father. Philippians 4:19 reads, "And *my God shall supply all your needs* according to His riches in glory by Christ Jesus" (emphasis mine).

So it becomes obvious that the first step toward mature faith is to make oneself aware of the presence and love of God in one's life. Setting out on the quest to build faith, we must begin at the cross, which is the greatest expression of the Father's love. It was there that the blood of Jesus was shed, and it was that blood that provides the way to the presence of the Father. His blood sacrifice, when accepted, retunes the heart to receive God's love, much like the dial on a radio can be tuned to receive a certain radio signal. We must accept that Jesus is "the Christ, the Son of the living God." This was Simon Peter's response to Jesus question, "But who do you say that I am?" (Matthew 16:15). If we acknowledge him as the Son of God who died for our sins and arose from the dead and later ascended to the throne of his Father, then we are in position to receive the Father's love.

Let us take this a step further in the interest of anyone who may be confronted, even now, by serious issues such as depression, loneliness, or major illness. You may be facing financial crisis or myriad other problems, and there may seem to be no way out. You may have arrived at that point in your life where you know there is nothing humanly possible that can be done. It is exactly here, under these conditions, that you are more likely to hear the words of Jesus, bidding you to come to him. He longs for you to receive your answer, and he delights in proving himself to you. When you turn to him and lay your problems at his feet, he will provide the answers that you need to overcome. As you see those problems dissolve before your very eyes, your faith will automatically take a giant step forward. The world may scream in your ear that the answer came through coincidence or an act of fate, but between you and your Lord, you will know better. As your faith grows, so will the excitement of locating new and fresh promises that are found in the Word of God and the wonderful experience of bringing his affirmations before him and watching those spiritual assurances become reality in the physical world. When there is a delay in receiving an answer, you will learn to wait in faith, confessing the promises of God's Word, content to wait upon him who is eternally faithful. Ultimately, you will come to the point where even if he does not answer as you might have chosen, his love will have become so precious that a seemingly unanswered prayer will have little to no effect. You will learn to rest in his will, realizing that his will is always for your good; he wants only the best for all of us who will trust in his Word.

We are given a measure of faith, according to Romans 12:3. When we first received Christ as Savior, we went from no faith to beginning faith very quickly. Through the revelation of the Holy Spirit, we became aware, first of all, that we were sinners and therefore in need of a Savior. Prior to that moment in our lives, we may have considered ourselves pretty good people. However, at that moment, we saw ourselves as God sees us—totally depraved and unclean and certainly in need of something that was beyond our human capabilities. That initial revelation continued by presenting Jesus as the perfect, sinless Son of God who was sacrificed to deliver us out of our defiled condition and to make us presentable to God. Let me add here that this revelatory experience, for some, might not occur suddenly but may happen over an extended period. In either case, the result is the same, for either way, we are united with the Father through the precious blood of his Son. The response to the revelation was made possible by this measure of faith, as recorded in Romans 12:3. There was no struggle to have faith after we received the revelation because we spontaneously knew that we were in the presence of truth. No matter how long it has been since that moment when we first realized that Jesus saved us for eternity, that experience continues to remain very real.

Let us digress for a moment and look at faith from a different perspective. We might ask ourselves, what is faith? I like *Webster's* definition because it is simple and to the point: "confidence or trust in a person or thing." At one time or another we all have heard the illustration that compares our faith in a chair's ability to hold us up to our faith in God. Our faith in the chair allows us to rest in the chair, much as our faith in God allows us to rest in God. While the analogy is basically good, there is always that possibility that the chair might have some structural defect that might cause it to collapse and take us to the floor with it.

Let us look at an illustration that will prove a little more stable. It might be said that faith is likened to gravity, for as gravity is an unseen force that holds us to earth, faith is an unseen force that binds us to God. However, this analogy is also inadequate to represent faith because when enough thrust and lift are applied, gravity also can be overcome. Nothing will ever triumph over faith, which works by love. Once we learn to walk in the love of our heavenly Father and his Son and the Holy Spirit, the faith that is spawned will inevitably subjugate any unbelief in their credibility. Just as those of us who were privileged to have been raised by honest and dependable parents and grandparents would defend their veracity, so we will become as we hear the Word of our heavenly Father disputed.

When we were introduced to the Lord, we did not have to struggle to have faith that we were sinners and that he had come to earth to be our Savior. Faith came easily on the heels of the revelation of who he was. When the Holy Spirit reveals truth to us through the Word of God, faith in that truth will always follow, and there will be no need for struggle.

When we first acknowledged Jesus as Savior, the Spirit of Christ came to dwell inside our human bodies. Romans 8:9 reads, "But ye are not in the flesh, but in the Spirit, if so be that the Spirit of God dwell in you. Now if any man have not the Spirit of Christ, he is none of his" (KJV). The first step toward receiving the revelation knowledge of God is to accept the truth of the blessed presence of the indwelling Spirit of Christ. Jesus told the disciples of the importance of the Spirit's coming, stating that there were many things he wished to tell them. They would be unable to understand, but "...when He, the Spirit of truth, has come, He will guide you into _all truth;_" (John 16:13, emphasis mine). The One who possesses *all* the knowledge that we need lives within every born-again believer, and he wants us to live our lives in light of that knowledge.

Teaching us to grow in faith is high on the Spirit's list of priorities because, remember, without faith it is impossible to please God. So let us look at this in a strictly rational sense. If the Spirit of Christ dwells within us and, as noted before, he possesses faith to heal the sick, feed the masses, and quiet the storm, then it stands to reason that this same faith resides within us. Right from the start, we are free from any struggle to obtain faith or, when once possessed, to maintain it. Our only obligation in the matter is to hear his Word and choose to agree with it. In fact, in Romans 10:17, Paul writes, "So then faith comes by hearing, and hearing by the word of God."

We can conclude that faith pleases God and disbelief displeases him. Why? Because faith is the vehicle by which we will come into the fullness of God's love. There are many born-again believers who have the Holy Spirit of Christ dwelling within them, but they have not advanced any further into a loving relationship with the Father than when they first came to know him. Sidelined by the deceptions of this world, many have long since given up any effort to seek God. Though the trappings of this world can be very attractive, they can never supplant the love of God. As mentioned earlier, he is that missing substance for which the soul of humankind yearns, that which will not be satisfied by physical things. If we desire to come into fellowship with him, we must use the key that has been provided—namely, faith.

In Numbers 13, we read the account of the children of Israel who arrived at the Jordan River, the last stage of their journey prior to entering into the land that God promised them for an inheritance. A little history is necessary here. God, through Moses, delivered his chosen people from approximately four hundred years of Egyptian slavery. They witnessed the complete annihilation of Pharaoh's army. They saw God perform multiple miracles throughout their journey to the land that God promised them. We know from Scripture that they were knowledgeable concerning the Land of Promise—this information was passed down through Abraham, Isaac, and Jacob. We learn from Genesis 50:24–25 that Joseph requested that his bones be buried in that Land of Promise. "And Joseph said to his brethren, 'I am dying; but God will surely visit you, and bring you out of this land unto the land which He swore to Abraham, to Isaac, and to Jacob.' Then Joseph took an oath from the children of Israel, saying, 'God will surely visit you, and you shall carry up my bones from here.'"

This knowledge, coupled with the many great miracles that God performed—especially the dividing of the Red Sea, the destruction of Pharaoh's army, and the miraculous provision of food and water—should have prepared them to take the land of Canaan. Conversely, they were about to participate in a show of disbelief in God's Word that was secondary only to that of Adam and Eve in the garden of Eden.

In Deuteronomy 11:22–24 KJV, we read God's promise. "For if ye shall diligently keep all these commandments which I commanded you, to do them, *to love the Lord your God, to walk in all his ways, and to cleave unto him*; then will the Lord drive out all these nations from before you, and ye shall possess greater nations and mightier than yourselves. *Every place whereon the soles of your feet shall tread shall be your's*: from the wilderness and Lebanon, from the river, the river Euphrates, even unto the uttermost sea shall your coast be" (emphasis mine).

We return now to the encampment of the children of Israel, which was located on the Jordan River directly across from the Promised Land. Moses had already sent out twelve spies, one from each of the tribes of Israel, to assess what lay before them in the new land. After forty days of searching, the spies returned with their findings and reported them to Moses, Aaron, and all the congregation of the children of Israel. All of the twelve spies had given glowing reports concerning the land. In Numbers 13:27, we read, "And they told him [Moses] and said, we came unto the land whither thou sentest us, and surely it floweth with milk and honey; and this is the fruit of it" (KJV). And they presented some of the fruit they had brought back from Canaan, one cluster of grapes so large that it took two men to carry it. But in Numbers 13:32–33 KJV, we read of the problem: "And they brought up an evil report of the land which they had searched unto the children of Israel, saying, the land, through which we have gone to search it, is a land that eateth up the inhabitants thereof; and all the people that we saw in it are men of a great stature. And there we saw the giants, the sons of Anak, which come of the giants: and we were in our own sight as grasshoppers, and so we were in their sight."

Only two of the spies, Joshua and Caleb, gave a positive report regarding the possibility of taking the land. They spoke words of agreement with God's Word found in Deuteronomy 11. In Numbers

14:8, we read their conclusion: "If the Lord delight in us, then he will bring us into this land, and give it us; a land which floweth with milk and honey" (KJV).

However, the congregation became so angry that they would have stoned Joshua and Caleb. In Numbers 14:10–11, we read God's immediate response: "And the glory of the Lord appeared in the tabernacle of the congregation before all the children of Israel. And the Lord said unto Moses, how long will this people provoke me? And how long will it be ere they *believe me*, for all the signs which I have shewed among them?" (KJV, emphasis mine).

Dropping down to Numbers 14:22–23, we read God's judgment: "Because all those men which have seen my glory, and my miracles, which I did in Egypt and in the wilderness, and have tempted me now these ten times, *and have not hearkened to my voice*; surely they shall not see the land which I swear unto their fathers, neither shall any of them that provoked me see it" (KJV, emphasis mine).

The eyes of the children of Israel saw the grapes, the milk and honey, and the fat of the land. And they were very impressed by the people who inhabited the land. In comparison to the giants of the land of Canaan, the children of Israel saw themselves as grasshoppers. We can sum this up by saying that except for Joshua and Caleb, the eyes of the congregation of the children of Israel were fixed on the things of this earth, the wealth of the land, the inhabitants of the land, and themselves. They had totally missed God's primary reason for bringing them to Canaan in the first place—*himself.* Having been engrossed with the earthly gifts that God delights in giving, they missed the fact that God was attempting to bring them back to himself. While it is true that all of their physical needs would have been abundantly met, that was not God's primary intent.

Had they focused on him, his love would have eradicated the fear of the giants by whom they were confronted. First John 4:18 tells us, "There is no fear in love; but perfect love casts out fear, because fear involves torment. But he who fears has not been made perfect in love." By placing their attention upon him, they would have been able to walk into the Land of Promise and take that land with ease. But with their eyes fixed on earthly goodies, they were only able to see undefeatable giants, and in comparison, they saw themselves as tiny insects.

This is exactly what takes place when we, as children of God, become enamored with the things of this life at the expense of fellowship with our loving Father. However, there is a difference. Even when we fail to enter into our promised land (a loving relationship with our Father, his Son, and the Holy Spirit), we can return to try again because of what Jesus accomplished at Golgotha. While experiencing the love of our Lord, no giant will ever stand in the way because "perfect love casts out fear." Without him, the giants (fear, guilt, depression, loneliness, illness, financial stress, etc.) that have plagued us will continue to prevent entrance into our promised land. But in the presence of almighty God, they cannot stand. Remember the passage of Scripture cited in Deuteronomy 11. God says that he will drive out all of the nations that inhabit the land. If we make the choice to enter into our promised land, he will do no less for us.

The children of Israel were condemned to a wilderness walk for forty years, never able to enter into the land of abundance, all because of lack of faith in God's Word. Forty years later, their descendents, under Joshua, returned to the Jordan River.

In Joshua 1:3, God repeats the pledge to Joshua that he had made to Moses: "Every place that the sole of your foot will tread upon I have given you, as I said to Moses." Yes, forty years later, after the generation of Moses's day had perished in the wilderness, Joshua, along with Caleb, led the children of Israel into the Promised Land. It is truly an unthinkable fact that the followers of Moses refused to enter Canaan because of fear of the giants. Let us cross over Jordan and listen to the voices of the giants of the Land of Promise through one of their own who was an eyewitness. In Joshua 2:9–11, we read:

> and she [Rahab] said unto the men [spies sent by Joshua to spy upon Jericho, the first obstacle to be

encountered upon crossing Jordan] know that the Lord hath given you the land, and that your terror is fallen upon us, and that all the inhabitants of the land *faint because of you*. For we have heard how the Lord dried up the water of the red sea for you, when ye came out Egypt; and what you did unto the two Kings of the Amorites, that were on the other side Jordan, Sihon and Og, whom you utterly destroyed. And as soon as we had heard these things, our hearts did melt, neither did there remain any more courage in any man [giants included], *because of you*: for the Lord your God, he is God in heaven above and in earth beneath. (KJV, emphasis mine)

This is our God—yours and mine—that Rahab is describing. The God who lives today with us is the same God who could have taken the original followers of Moses into the Promised Land. Hebrews 13:8 reads, "Jesus Christ is the same yesterday, and today, and forever." It is just as unthinkable for us today as it was for Moses's followers that we would allow ourselves to be intimidated by anything that would attempt to prevent us from following our God anywhere that he might choose to lead us. He is just as capable and as willing to destroy our giants today, if we simply choose to have *faith* in him.

Hebrews 11:1 reads, "Now faith is the substance of things hoped for, the evidence of things not seen." As a child growing up in southern Georgia, I was very close with my grandfather. We both enjoyed most outdoor activities, such as fishing and hunting. My grandfather was one of those men who never failed to tell the truth. If he promised to take me on a fishing trip, I could always count on the fact that we were, without question, going fishing. The excitement brought on by the anticipation of the fishing trip was as enjoyable as the trip itself. My anticipation was part and parcel of the trip. My faith in the coming event became like "substance" because I knew, beyond a shadow of a doubt, that the fishing trip was forthcoming. At seventy-six years of age, I now have had the pleasure of spending far more time with my heavenly Father than I ever did with my earthly grandfather. In that time, I have learned to trust him and what he says with even greater assurance than that which I placed in my grandfather's word.

Hebrews 11 contains the faith hall of fame, a collection of biblical giants of the faith. Though there isn't space to mention all of them, I would be remiss if I did not discuss Abraham, whom I consider the father of those who walk in faith. When Abram left Ur of the Chaldees, he had no knowledge of where he was going. God had spoken to him, and he set out in faith in what God had said. In Genesis 12:1–3, we read, "Get out of your country, from your family and from your father's house, to a land that I will show you. I will make you a great nation; I will bless you and make your name great; and you shall be a blessing. I will bless those who bless you, and I will curse him who curses you; and in you all the families of the earth shall be blessed." As we read this Scripture, the tendency is to think that Abram might have left his home and kin in search of the promised earthly blessing, but I believe that Abram left Ur in search of the God who had promised the blessing. We read from Hebrews 11:10, "For he [Abraham] looked for a city which hath foundations, whose builder and maker is God" (KJV). Abraham, as he was known later, sought God.

God's blessing, recorded in Genesis 12, had promised to make a great nation through Abraham. When Abraham and his wife, Sarah, were far past the age of childbearing, God finally honored his promise by allowing Sarah to conceive and bear a child, Isaac. This elderly man of approximately one hundred years of age had maintained his faith in God's promise. There had been one time when Abraham, attempting to help God fulfill his promise, produced a child through Hagar, one of his bond servants, but most of his life had been a consistent walk of faith, even to the point of willingness to sacrifice his only son, Isaac, at God's request. Because of his great faith in God, Abraham was abundantly blessed.

We cannot fail to mention David, who in his teens slew the giant Goliath by faith. First Samuel 17:45 gives us the picture of David, standing before mighty Goliath, with a slingshot and a few stones. David said to the Philistine giant, "You come to me with a sword, with a spear, and with a javelin. But I come to you in the name of the Lord of hosts, the God of the armies of Israel, whom you have defied." God, who is the same yesterday, today, and forever, stood in the valley of Elah with this young shepherd boy, just as he had walked with Joshua into the land of Canaan and just as he will walk with us as we face our giants today. David went on to become king and to perform great exploits, but the obvious desire of his heart was to be close to his God. You have but to read his psalms to know that David lived to be with God, and he was a man after God's own heart. In Psalm 37:4, he writes, "Delight yourself also in the Lord; and he shall give you the desires of your heart." And in Psalm 16:11, we read, "You will show me the path of life; in Your presence is fullness of joy; at Your right hand are pleasures for evermore." Though many psalms describe David's relationship with the Lord, I will end this by using the last verse of the highly quoted Psalm 23: "Surely goodness and mercy shall follow me all the days of my life; and *I will dwell in the house of the Lord forever*" (emphasis mine). David was a great king and a skilled general and was much beloved by his people, but with all of his successes in this world, David preferred the pleasures that were found in the presence of his God.

The Bible teaches us of Noah and his ark, which he built by faith. From the Scripture, we learn of Jacob, who was so determined because of his faith that he wrestled with God. Joseph, by faith, arose from slave to viceroy in Egypt. Daniel was confined in a lion's den because of his faith. Joshua, by faith, fought the battle of Jericho and conquered the Promised Land. Shadrach, Meshach, and Abednego, by faith, refused to bow to Nebuchadnezzar, and a host of others including Queen Esther, Samson, and Gideon lived by faith in God. Job revealed his determination to remain faithful to his God no matter what suffering he might have had to endure. And the list goes on and on to include John the Baptist, Peter, Paul, and Stephen, but the greatest faith of all was evident in the life of Jesus. This was the faith that was sacrificed at the cross in order that he might take upon himself all of those sins of doubt and unbelief committed by humankind, from Adam and Eve to the last sin that will be committed prior to his return.

During Jesus's earthly ministry, he had an occasion to cross the Sea of Galilee with his disciples. In Mark 4:35, he said to his disciples, "Let us pass over unto the other side" (KJV). Some time passed before a great storm erupted, the waves roaring, so that the ship appeared to be filling with water. Jesus was asleep in the back of the ship, so the disciples awakened him, and he proceeded to rebuke the wind, also speaking to the sea, "Peace, be still." Immediately, the wind ceased, and there was a great calm. Because the disciples had been so afraid during the storm, Jesus questioned them. "Why are you so fearful? How is it that you have *no* faith?" (Mark 4:40, emphasis mine). That must have been a powerful storm to have disturbed the disciples, many of whom were fishermen and acquainted with storms at sea. Most of us would have had the same reaction as the disciples, so we might ask the question, why should Jesus be as sharp with the disciples as he seems to have been? However, when we examine what Jesus had said before they embarked on their sailing journey, we might better understand his reaction. The Word of God, spoken from the mouth of Jesus, had said, "Let us pass over unto the other side." Therefore, the truth of the matter was that Jesus and the disciples were going to pass over to the other side, no matter what circumstances—including powerful storms—might have arisen. Jesus, having said this, could sleep because his faith was flawless. The disciples had said to him in Mark 4:38 KJV, "Master, carest thou not that we perish?" In his response to their query, he could have reprimanded them for doubting his love for them, but he chided them by using the words *no faith*, which was the equivalent of saying, "You know that I love you, and you must know that I have no desire to see you perish. As long as I am here, you shall not perish, whether I am asleep or not." The truth is when Jesus said, "Let us go to the other side," nothing on earth or in hell itself could have stopped him or his disciples from reaching the other shore.

He spoke to others of their *little faith*, but only twice did he speak of *great faith*. On one occasion, he spoke those words in response to the faith of a Canaanite woman who had approached him in an attempt to coax him into healing her daughter. The daughter, according to Matthew 15:22, was "severely demon possessed." Jesus at first resisted, stating, "It is not good to take the children's bread and throw it to the little dogs." Jesus was testing this lady by telling her that since he was a Jew and had come to minister to the children of Israel that he should not bestow the benefits of his ministry upon Gentiles. But this lady would not be dissuaded. She persisted, stating, "Yes, Lord, yet even the little dogs eat the crumbs which fall from their master's table" (Matthew 15:27). Jesus's response is recorded in Matthew 15:28, which reads, "O woman, *great is your faith!* Let it be to you as you desire" (emphasis mine). Her daughter was then made whole.

The other occasion on which Jesus mentioned great faith is found in Matthew 8. A Roman centurion approached Jesus to ask him to heal his paralyzed servant. Jesus agreed to go to the centurion's home and heal the servant, but the Roman responded, "Lord, I am not worthy that you should come under my roof. But only speak the word, and my servant will be healed" (Matthew 8:8). When Jesus heard the rejoinder by the centurion, "He marveled, and said to those who followed, 'assuredly, I say to you, I have not found such *great faith*, not even in Israel!'" (Matthew 8:10, emphasis mine). In both cases, the key figures were Gentiles. Otherwise, there seems to be no similarity between the two. Among the Jewish people, especially the religious hierarchy, Jesus encountered a great deal of resistance to his ministry. He could not find the same kind of faith that he saw in these two Gentiles. Somehow, the Jewish religion of Jesus's day seems to have had an immunizing effect on its adherents, so they could not receive the truth—that the Son of God had come to earth and was present in their midst. God himself, in the flesh, walked and talked with them. Hard, cold religion, whether of that day or the present, that does not teach faith in a relationship with a loving God is as useless as an icemaker at the North Pole. It is as "Sounding brass or a tinkling cymbal" and will, inevitably, dampen the fire of the most enthusiastic in his or her pursuit of a relationship with the Lord.

The Evil One is well aware that as long as the believer is in a position to experience the love of God, he is undefeatable. However, if the Devil can create even the slightest doubt in the heart of the child of God concerning the Father's great love, then the shield of faith will be breached. Just as the mighty dam might crumble as the result of a small, unrepaired leak, so can the believer be defeated by the smallest crack in his faith shield. It is even more important that we guard against defects in those pieces of armor that protect vital areas. This is why the apostle Paul emphasized the shield of faith when describing the armor of the believer. Let us look again at Ephesians 6:16, in which he writes, "...*above all*, taking the shield of faith with which you will be able to quench all the fiery darts of the wicked one" (emphasis mine).

In battle, I may lose my helmet or breastplate, but if I have the ability to use my shield to block the arrow that is coming at me, then I can live to fight another day. This is why it is essential that we maintain our faith by setting aside time to be alone with the Lord and by studying and meditating upon his Word, especially those Scriptures that emphasize his loving care for us. It might be a little difficult for that person who is just beginning in his or her walk with the Lord, but as we continue, there will be progress toward that end we seek. In time, these efforts will become second nature to us, and we will long for that quiet time in which we can fully experience his marvelous love. The experience of the quiet time will expand and overlap into various other routines of the day, giving us the benefit of realizing his continuing presence with us.

Of course, Satan will attempt to distract us through the various cares of this world. This is where it becomes incumbent upon the believer to refuse those thoughts, memories, imaginations, or emotions that disagree with God's Word. In John 14:27, Jesus places the responsibility upon the believer for maintaining the peace that he has given us: "Peace I leave with you. My peace I give to you; not as the world gives do I give to you. *Let not your heart be troubled neither let it be afraid*" (emphasis mine). Instead of praying so much for peace, though this is a noble practice, let us begin to walk in the peace that we already have been given. We have to learn to refuse toxic thoughts, memories, imaginations, and emotions that disturb our peace if we are to keep our hearts from being troubled or afraid.

You can rest assured that anything that disturbs your peace, which has been given you by Christ himself, did not come from God. That noxious thought or memory that can produce feelings of poor self-esteem must be subjected to the scrutiny of God's Word. We must take control of this thinking by learning to counter with the truth of God's Word, which tells us that we are highly esteemed by our gracious Father who loves us. The antidote for any poisonous thought or event can be found in the Word of God. We must find those Scriptures and use them.

I would encourage those of you who may be struggling with problems that seem insurmountable to remember that with God, all things are possible. When we began our journey with the Lord, we were much like the disciples who stood with him on the shores of the Sea of Galilee, when he spoke these words: "Let us pass over unto the other side." Like Abraham, we may not know where the other side is located or what awaits us there, but we can rest assured that we will pass over unto the other side. We can also be certain that through it all, Jesus will never leave us alone. Remember Hebrews 13:5—"*I will never leave you nor forsake you.*" Storms will come, as will the quiet doldrums, but we will always hear his voice if we listen carefully. "Let not your heart be troubled."

May we never forget the price that Jesus paid in order to make faith in him the way to eternal life. Without his cross, we would be forced to live under a rigid system of laws, our salvation dependent upon our own ability to live up to the standards set forth by them. But he took the sins of Adam's disbelief and that of all who have followed and now proclaims to all who will hear, *If you believe in me, you shall never perish but have eternal life.*

In Jesus, we have the potential for a triumphant life and victory over Satan and over our minds, from which all defeatist attitudes and emotions arise. Paul writes in 2 Corinthians 2:14, "Now thanks be to God who always leads us in triumph in Christ, and through us diffuses the fragrance of his knowledge in every place." This victory cannot be obtained through our achievements any more than we could obtain salvation by our efforts. It is not about us or what we can do; it is about Jesus and his accomplishments at the cross. If necessary, let us scream the following toward any opposition, whether the Devil, this world in which we live, or especially to our own minds: "It is not about me; it is about Jesus and his obedience at the cross."

First John 5:4–5 reads, "For whatever is born of God overcomes the world. And this is the victory that has overcome the world—our faith. Who is he who overcomes the world, but he who believes that Jesus is the Son of God?" We are expected to be overcomers; God sent his son to die in order to make it possible, and if we do not receive the victory, we devalue that which was accomplished by Jesus at the cross.

But if we apply faith to the promises of victory that are contained in the Word of God, we will see triumph in our individual lives. In Jesus's own words, recorded in Mark 11:22–24, we read, "So Jesus answered and said to them, <u>have faith in God</u> for assuredly, I say to you, whoever says to this mountain, 'be removed and be cast into the sea,' and does not doubt in his heart, but <u>believes</u> that those things he says will be done, he will have whatever he says. Therefore I say to you, whatsoever things you ask when you pray, <u>believe</u> that you receive them and you will have them" (emphasis mine).

This great promise is ours and can be manifested in our lives if we develop our faith. There is only one hitch. When we come before the Father, we must come without unforgiveness. Jesus continues in Mark 11:25–26, "And whenever you stand praying, if you have anything against anyone, forgive him, that your Father in heaven may also forgive you your trespasses. But if you do not forgive, neither will your Father In heaven forgive your trespasses." This major hurdle to the victorious life must be negotiated. We simply cannot allow unforgiveness, for something that happened to us in the past, to rob us of a beautiful life in the Lord. No one on the face of this planet has ever been more mistreated than Jesus was at the cross, yet he could say, "Father forgive them for they know not what they do" (Luke 23:34 KJV). His obedience to the Father's will outweighed any need or desire for spite or revenge. The glory of the relationship with the Father superseded any need to hold a grudge, even as the Romans plunged those spikes into his hands and feet. The same should be true of us as we seek a close relationship with our heavenly Father. Though the stronghold of unforgiveness may seem unbreakable, if we choose to forgive in order to have his victorious life, and we confess it for what it is and then place it under captivity to his obedience (2 Corinthians 10:4), it will be pulled down.

The Lord wills that all of us simply choose to remove those hindrances and walk in him. In these last days, the cause of Christ needs men and women like the prophet Elijah, who, when confronted with the powers of darkness arrayed against him, stood in faith in his God and called down fire from heaven to prove the existence of the one true God. In 1 Kings 18:21, we read, "And Elijah came to all the people, and said, 'how long will you falter between two opinions? If the Lord is God, follow him; but if Baal, follow him.' But the people answered him not a word." Pitted against the 450 profits of Baal, all of whom were determined to display the power of their god, Elijah challenged them to a duel between Jehovah and Baal. God Almighty answered the prayer of Elijah the prophet, and fire rained from heaven to destroy Elijah's sacrifice. After beholding this display of fire from heaven, the people rallied behind the man of God, and the false prophets of Baal were slain. If the world ever needed someone to stand in faith for fire (power) from heaven, that time is upon us.

Do I think that this could happen in our day? Yes, because our God is the same God to whom Elijah prayed. Though Elijah obviously had the Holy Spirit of God upon him, that same Spirit that raised Jesus from the dead is alive inside us. The power that overcame death, hell, and the grave is within us and only requires acknowledgment by faith to be effective. Child of God, awaken to that which is within you, and, in faith, ask the Holy Spirit to reveal himself.

We then take up our crosses by refusing to defend ourselves. By developing faith in the presence of God, we come to realize his proficiency in dealing with our enemies, whether they be spiritual or physical. Consequently, by refusing to defend ourselves, we open the door to his protection. As long as we attempt to protect ourselves, we handcuff our God. Many try to wield both—this shield of self-defense and this shield of the Spirit—but the hand will only hold one shield at a time; therefore, neither can be optimally effective.

An example of this is the tendency to reduce the intensity of our self-defense precisely because we are Christian. In other words, thinking it is unchristian, we refuse to mount an adequate defense of ourselves. This then creates a state where an attempt at self-defense is half-hearted, and since spiritual defense is practically nonexistent, there can be little hope of victory. Hence, we must determine to lay down the shield of self-defense, and by so doing, we take up the cross. By removing the shield of self-defense, our hands are free to take up the shield of faith.

O Lord, wash us in the blood that flowed from the hand of Jesus, which he allowed to be nailed to the cross that we might take

CHAPTER 6

THE SWORD

Gird thy sword upon thy thigh, O most mighty,
with thy glory and thy majesty.

—Psalm 45:3

During Christ's ministry on this earth, the forces of Satan manifested
an awareness of Jesus's true identity. A prime example of this is found
in Matthew 8:28–29, which reads, "When He had come to the other
side, to the country of the Gergesenes, there met Him two demon-
possessed men, coming out of the tombs, exceedingly fierce, so that
no one could pass that way. And suddenly they cried out, saying,
what have we to do with You, Jesus, You Son of God? Have You
come here to torment us before the time?" This event provides a
particularly clear window into the spiritual world and the adversarial
role of our Enemy. It is also quite clear that these agents of Satan
also realized and respected his authority over them, for in Matthew
8:30–31, we read, "Now a good way off from them there was a herd
of many swine feeding. So the demons begged Him [Jesus], saying,
if You cast us out, permit us to go away into the herd of swine."

Those same forces must have frolicked around the cross that day
at Golgotha, realizing that they were about to witness the death of the
One who had called himself "the way, the truth, and the life" (John

14:6). The Way to the salvation of all humankind, the truth of God's love for humankind, and the life himself was dying on a Roman cross. The powers of darkness must have held high celebration that day when Jesus was crucified, but in their triumphant revelry, they could never have envisioned God's masterfully crafted plan that was to spell their doom. The master of deceit and father of lies, along with all of his forces, was about to be out-manipulated by the Father of truth.

It is incomprehensible that while he was being crucified, Jesus took upon himself all of the deception and falsehood of fallen humankind, from Adam until the time when he will return to this earth to establish his millennial kingdom. Jesus took the lies of this world upon himself, and when the dust settled at the cross, humankind no longer had to live in the darkness of satanic deceitfulness. In receiving by faith the complete work of the Son of God at the cross, Jesus himself became and would forever be our Light. Illuminated by his brilliance, the believer will be capable of walking through a world of darkness by the revelatory knowledge and wisdom of his Holy Spirit. The child of God can only be deceived if he or she allows it to happen by ignoring the function of the Holy Spirit, who abides within each of us. Proverbs 3:5–6 reads, "Trust in the Lord with all your heart, and lean not on your own understanding; in all your ways acknowledge Him, and He shall direct your paths."

We have seen that through the power of the blood of Jesus, a way has been established that we might return to the courts of our loving heavenly Father. As his children, we have been given a *crown* and *helmet* by Jesus, who sacrificed his own heavenly crown for us. He also provided a *robe* for us when he allowed his Roman executioners to remove his own robe. He relinquished his sovereign faith, which could have easily extricated him from the bondage of the Romans, thus allowing himself to be manhandled and pinned to a cruel cross, that we might have a *shield of faith*. Jesus also provided a *sword* (our offensive weapon), the Word of God (the truth).

For that moment in time known as Calvary, Jesus sacrificed his status as *truth* and took upon himself all of the lies of the world. All of the lying, the cheating, and the fraud of this world was placed upon him—absolute truth personified. In allowing this extreme miscarriage of justice, he bestowed upon us the capability of walking in the truth. It is the truth that will make us free, just as, initially, the lie of Satan enslaved all of humankind through Adam. Jesus said, "If you abide in My word, you are My disciples indeed. And you shall know the truth, and the truth shall make you free" (John 8:31–32). Lying serves as the foundation for all of Satan's prisons; consequently, whatever imprisons the believer will be removed if the truth of God is applied to it. Remember Isaiah's prophecy recorded in Isaiah 61, concerning Jesus's coming to this world. One of the reasons for which he left his heavenly kingdom is explained here: "To proclaim liberty to the captives, and the opening of the prison to them that are bound" (KJV).

You see, the kingdom of Satan exists in darkness and deception, and the only way that he can imprison anyone is through deception. In John 8:44, Jesus confronted the Pharisees, who obviously had been beguiled by Satan's seductiveness, "You are of your father the devil, and the desires of your father you want to do. *He was a murderer from the beginning and does not stand in the truth because there is no truth in him. When he speaks a lie, he speaks from his own resources for he is a liar and the father of it*" (emphasis mine). Ephesians 6 tells us that he *rules* in darkness. Jesus substantiates this claim by calling him the prince of this world in John 12:31 KJV. Since the cross, however, the only power that the prince of this world can bring to bear upon the believer is that which the believer will allow. Satan was totally defeated at the cross!

It was into this world of darkness, ruled by the father of lies, that Jesus came to set the captive free. Although the world staggers along in darkness, blinded by the deception of the Evil One, the Light sent from God is truly available to anyone who will hear. In contrast to the darkness of this world and the Devil, John casts Jesus as the Light. John 1:4–9, reads, "In Him was life, and the life was the light of men. And the light shines in the darkness, and the darkness did not comprehend it. There was a man sent from God, whose name was John [John the Baptist]. This man came for a witness, to bear witness of the Light, that all through him might believe. He was not that Light, but was sent to bear witness of that Light. That was the true Light which gives light to every man coming in to the world." As believers, we have seen the light of Christ, but we walk in a world that continues to be deceived by the powers of darkness. Because we have received this light and the Holy Spirit to navigate for us through this treacherous world of darkness, we should give continual thanks. For though the world functions in darkness, we are told in James 1:17, "Every good gift and every perfect gift is from above, and comes down from the Father of *lights*, with whom there is no variation or shadow of turning" (emphasis mine).

Now we can see that he sacrificed his truth when he took upon himself all the falsehoods of humankind and, by so doing, made the truth available to us. It is the truth that will make us free, just as the lies of Satan caused us to be enslaved. Jesus prayed, concerning us, in John 17:15–17, "I do not pray that You should take them out of the world, but that You should keep them from the evil one. They are not of the world, just as I am not of the world. Sanctify them by Your truth. *Your word is truth*" (emphasis mine). It is through the truth of God's Word that we are freed from bondage. Again, looking to the words of our Lord Jesus himself, which are recorded in John 8:31–32, we read, "If you abide in My word, you are My disciples indeed. And you shall know the truth, and the truth shall make you free." The application of truth to the walls of any prison having deceit as its foundation will result in freedom for any who might be imprisoned within. Satanic strongholds are based upon falsehood and are inevitably forced to crumble when confronted by truth, even as darkness cannot exist when light is applied. To this world, lost in the darkness of satanic deception, we should shout the praises of our Savior who has so graciously provided us with his truth.

Realizing that the Word of God is the divine repository for truth, let us focus our attention on the purposes for its existence and the methods by which it should be employed. In Hebrews 4:12, we read, "For the word of God is living and powerful and sharper than any two-edged sword, piercing even to the division of soul and spirit, and of joints and marrow, and is a discerner of the thoughts and intents of the heart." And in Ephesians 6:17, "And take the helmet of salvation, and *the sword of the Spirit, which is the word of God...*" (emphasis mine). The prophecy concerning the Messiah in Isaiah 49:2 likens his mouth to a sharp sword. At the battle of Armageddon, when Jesus leads the hosts of heaven to this earth, Revelation 19:15 tells us, "Now out of His mouth goes a sharp *sword*, that with it He should strike the nations." Here we are told that we should take up the sword, the Word of God, as an offensive weapon. The truth is that the world was created by the Word of God, and it is true that the nations opposing Christ at Armageddon will be smitten by the word that comes forth from the mouth of Jesus. Should this not then cause us to wonder in awe at the power of this sword, which has been placed at our disposal?

Remember that at his arraignment, Jesus had to remain silent in order to allow his trial and ultimate conviction to proceed. The words, had they been spoken, would have most probably prevented his crucifixion. Just as he laid down his shield of protection in allowing one hand to be nailed to the cross, he also gave up his sword (the power of his Word), allowing the Roman soldiers to nail his other hand to the cross. In so doing, he not only made it possible for us to have salvation and a life of victory by *faith*, but he also provided our only offensive weapon, the Word of God. Just as the shield allows the soldier to block an enemy's thrusts, the sword allows him to strike back at his assailant.

In addition, we have the Holy Spirit within to lead the way in the battle. Ephesians 6 speaks of the Word of God as the sword of the Spirit. When we realize the awesome power of the sword (the Word), spoken in faith (the shield) under the authoritative power of the Holy Spirit, we will have a positive effect not only in our own lives but also in the world around us. Jesus himself led the way in revealing this to us during his sojourn in the wilderness, when he was confronted by Satan. At no time during any one of the three confrontations with the Evil One did Jesus call down angels, or invoke his status as prince of heaven, or use any form of violence. He simply rebutted Satan on each occasion with Scripture (the sword of truth). Just as certainly as the Devil fled from Jesus, if we, in faith, resist him in the same manner, he will also flee. James 4:7 reads, "Therefore submit to God. Resist the devil and *he will flee from you*" (emphasis mine). Luke 10:19 reads, "Behold, I give you authority to trample on serpents and scorpions, and *over all the power of the enemy*, and nothing shall by any means hurt you" (emphasis mine).

Without a doubt, the Scriptures teach that Satan is defeated and that we have been given power to defeat him in our own lives, but if we do not follow the advice of James and actively resist him, he remains a powerful force who is capable of producing disastrous effects upon our lives, even unto death. We must positively understand that any power given to us is only available through the guidance of the Holy Spirit and the Word of God. First Peter 5:8 reads, "Be sober, be vigilant; because your adversary the devil walks about like a roaring lion, seeking whom he may devour." And Paul tells us in Ephesians 6:12, "For we do not wrestle against flesh and blood, but against principalities, against powers, against the rulers of the darkness of this age, against spiritual hosts of wickedness in the heavenly places." In other words, we are in a battle in which we have the advantage because of what Jesus made available for us on the cross. However, if we choose to ignore the truth of God's Word and willingly go on walking in the darkness of Satan's deception, we will never gain the victory and never walk in the abundant life that the Word of God promises.

Following Paul's admonitions, which are recorded in Ephesians 6, we must gird our loins about with truth. So far, I discussed truth from the standpoint of the sword of the Spirit, which is the Word of God. Now let us look at the belt of truth. Just as a natural belt encircles the body to hold up the trousers, so the belt of truth girds us by supporting victorious life in Christ. Everything in the Christian life is founded upon truth. All the truths of God's Word (the sword of the Spirit) rest in the scabbard, which must hang from the belt of truth. As Christians, everything in our lives, whether in battle or at rest, depends upon the truth of God's Word. Just as the trousers fall without a belt, so goes victorious life in Christ without the girdle of truth, which supports the scabbard, which holds the sword of the Spirit, which is the Word of God.

Let us return to the cross to be washed again in the blood of Jesus that was so lovingly shed on our behalf. When we assented to the fact that Jesus, the carpenter's son from Nazareth, was truly the Son of almighty God, we set ourselves up for another question of great importance to the follower of Christ. Is the Bible the inerrant truth, delivered through divine inspiration to man by the Creator? Many who call themselves Christians argue that there are contradictions within its pages, and some say that entire books contained within its covers should be deleted, replacing them with other writings, such as the Gnostic Gospels. Some declare that there may have been errors in translation, citing the unequivocal fact that certain translations contain disagreements. While their proposals appear to have some seemingly rational value, it is, however, irrational to me to claim that a perfect God would deliver an imperfect message to his children. He is definitely not the author of confusion, and he would never seek to mislead those who call him Father. Though there are seemingly minor differences between some translations, the divine intent seems to be preserved. Any apparent differences are completely overshadowed by the multiple consistencies that have been maintained over thousands of years and through many translations. This, to me, provides ample and irrefutable evidence of divine determination to preserve scriptural integrity. I bring this up only to caution the reader to be aware of possible satanic influence where confidence in God's Word is concerned. We have but to remember that the integrity of God's Word was the very issue that brought about the fall of Adam and Eve in the first place. By partaking of the forbidden fruit, Adam had proclaimed God's Word to be untrue. Jesus, speaking to the Father, stated in John 17:17, "Your word is truth."

Can we maintain growth toward victorious, abundant life when confronted with the cares and trials of life on this earth? Yes, but the ultimate answer to this question will be determined by how prudent we are in our attitude toward the Word of God. This is readily seen in Mark 4. Here, Jesus reveals just how crucial the Word is in maintaining a close relationship with the Lord, which is synonymous with an abundant life in Christ. In Mark 4, Jesus explains to the disciples why some people fail. Mark 4:14 reads, "The sower sows the word." In Mark 4:15, he continues, "When they hear, Satan comes immediately and takes away the word that was sown in their hearts." This first group, seed, which is dropped by the wayside, makes no progress at all because the truth of God's Word is quickly removed by the Enemy.

The second category of believer receives the Word with gladness. Mark 4:17 reads, "...and they have no root in themselves, and so endure only for a time. Afterward, when tribulation or persecution arises for the word's sake, immediately they stumble." This group is represented by those where the Word has been sown on stony ground, and they are destined to failure because they have developed shallow roots. They start fast, but because their root structure is so inadequate, they are unable to create a solid foundation for further growth. The third category is represented by the seed sown among thorns. The meaning of the thorns is spelled out: "And the cares of this world, the deceitfulness of riches, and the desires for other things entering in choke the word, and it becomes unfruitful" (Mark 4:19). It can be very difficult at times to prevent ourselves from falling into this third category. With the many cares that are thrown at us every day and living in a world moving at a breakneck pace, life can threaten to overwhelm. I believe that most Christians fail in their attempts to live the abundant life because of the issues that are faced by this group. Jesus tells us why failure occurs; the Word is "choked." This choking of the Word occurs because of deceit. Although Satan is not mentioned here, as he is in the first category, he is nonetheless at work; he is the father of deceit. Most of the problems in our lives today have their origins in the "lust of other things," which is motivated by the "deceitfulness of riches." As has been discussed, the things of this world will never bring peace or satisfy the longing for a life with God. We have been deceived into thinking that material things will supplant our need for God because this is all that the master of deception has to offer. If we would move into the fourth level (those who bring forth fruit), we must resist the Evil One and yield ourselves to the Holy Spirit, who is always present to guide us into a relationship with the Lord.

Is it any wonder that Satan attempts to remove or choke the Word, seeing that it is that same truth that will defeat him if allowed to grow? Then, in light of this truth, we should be determined to read, memorize, meditate, quote, and, above all, *stand on the word of truth*. Every time we speak it in faith, whether from memory or reading, he will flee. Oh yes, he will try again and again, but if we are persistent, we will triumph in the end (2 Corinthians 2:14). Remember he tempted Jesus, the Son of God, three times.

We can say, without equivocation, that truth repels Satan and all of his forces, as a light repels darkness. When we walk into a dark room and switch on a light, the darkness is eradicated immediately. Darkness cannot return until we choose to flip the switch off. In the same way, the kingdom of darkness cannot remain where the light of the truth of God's Word is spoken by faith. We are told in Ephesians 6 that we wrestle with the rulers of the *darkness* of this world, whose purpose it is to steal, kill, and destroy, but—praise the Lord—our Father has "...qualified us to be partakers of the inheritance of the Saints in the *light. He has delivered us from the power of darkness* and conveyed us into the kingdom of the Son of His love" (Colossians 1:12–13, emphasis mine). First Peter 2:9 reads, "But you are a chosen generation, a royal priesthood, a holy nation, His own special people, that you may proclaim the praises of Him *who called you out darkness into His marvelous light*" (emphasis mine). Jesus came as a light into a world of darkness.

While it is true that we have been translated from a kingdom of darkness into the kingdom of light, we must continue to live in a world controlled by the rulers of darkness. This does not mean that we are controlled by darkness, for we have been empowered by the Holy Spirit to live in light and truth. He will teach us to discern evil when in its presence, and he will reveal to us the power of God's Word (the truth) to defeat that evil.

Deceitfulness has become rampant in our society. We have arrived at the point where few people trust our political leadership in Washington. Every few minutes, our minds are bombarded with commercials on TV that promise far more than their product could ever deliver. As a society, we are on the verge of accepting student cheating on exams as a "cool" thing to do. Some say that it shows imagination and the ability to think on one's feet. I do not wish to belabor this point; if you have lived in this country for the last twenty years or so, you know the trend.

The Bible teaches that falsehood and deception are signs that will mark the time just prior to the return of Christ. This is especially true in all things related to Christianity. Matthew 24:24 tells us, "For false christ's and false prophets will rise and show great signs and wonders to deceive, if possible, even the elect." In this world, only the light of God's truth will stand against satanic deception; therefore, it is absolutely necessary that we learn to walk in spiritual truth and light.

It is very interesting to note that when Jesus returns to set up his millennial kingdom, Satan will be bound for a period of one thousand years. Revelation 20:1–3 reads, "Then I saw an angel coming down from heaven, having the key to the bottomless pit and a great chain in his hand. He laid hold of the dragon, that serpent of old, who is the Devil and Satan, and bound him for a thousand years; and he cast him into the bottomless pit, and shut him up, and set a seal on him, so that he should *deceive the nations no more till the thousand years were finished*" (emphasis mine). And when the thousand years expires, Satan will be released. According to Revelation 20:8, he "*will go out to deceive the nations* which are in the four corners of the earth, Gog and Magog, to gather them together to battle, whose number is as the sand of the sea" (emphasis mine). He is the Father of Lies, and there is no truth in him. He comes to steal, kill, and destroy, and deception is the method by which he achieves his goal.

In the garden of Eden, Adam and Eve were deceived by Satan into believing that God had lied to them about the consequences of eating the forbidden fruit. The modus operandi of the Father of Lies is much the same today; it has not changed since it was used against the first family. God's Word is the only offensive weapon in the believer's arsenal and the only weapon on this planet with power enough to defeat the Evil One and the powers of darkness. Many are so caught up in fighting what is perceived as the enemy (flesh and blood) that they miss the real Enemy. This weapon of ours must be utilized in the spiritual realm, where its power has great effect against Satan's forces. If we continue to fight windmills, as did Don Quixote, we will ultimately lose the battle. But if we determine to employ our weapon (the spoken Word) against the real enemy (the forces of Satan), the victory will be ours, and we will reap the benefits of this spiritual triumph in the natural realm.

Let us take this discussion a step further. We cannot separate truth from Jesus, for just as the Evil One is a liar, Jesus is the truth. He declared himself to be the truth in John 14:6. John 1:1 calls him the word and ascribes to him equality with the Father. This loving word of truth (Jesus) will become, through the written Word of truth, a real presence in our lives, if we are willing for the Holy Spirit to reveal him within its pages.

Sadly, many born-again Christians are much like Cleopus, one of those who traveled to Emmaus from Jerusalem following the death of Jesus. Grief-stricken over the loss of the one they had supposed to be the Messiah and apparently under the assumption that the cause of Christ was finished, they made their way home, their dreams crushed. Satan, Rome, and the Sanhedrin in Jerusalem had won. There seemed to be no anticipation of the triumphant resurrection prophesied by Jesus. In Matthew 27:63, we see that the Pharisees were well aware that Jesus had said that he would arise from the dead after three days, but these followers of Jesus seemed to have dismissed this possibility. As we read Luke's account of this event, we can sense only despair and discouragement (Luke 24:13–33).

The Bible tells us that as these travelers made their way home, Jesus drew near to them, but they did not recognize him. It is very interesting that they did not immediately realize their companion was Jesus. It is my firm belief that herein lies the key to victory in the Christian life. It is a sad, sad thing when we who are called by his name cannot recognize his presence with us any better than these travelers on the road to Emmaus, even though we have the Holy Spirit within us and the New Testament before us. Jesus realized that those residents of Emmaus were incapable of identifying him as they walked along together, and just as certainly, he is aware that we today are not conscious of his presence in our lives much of the time.

Why didn't Jesus simply walk up to his followers and tell them who he was? Personally, I believe that Jesus used this encounter with these travelers to teach future generations of followers how to realize fully his presence in their lives.

The entire account of the events, which occurred on the Emmaus road, are included in Luke 24:13–33. Let us begin in verse 27, where we read, "And beginning at Moses and all the prophets, He expounded to them in all the Scriptures *the things concerning Himself*" (emphasis mine). In other words, he spoke to them of himself from the Scripture (the Word of truth). He did not perform a miracle, preach, or prophesy but attempted to reveal himself through the Word. It is this same sword of the Spirit, the Word of God taught by the Spirit of God, that will eradicate the darkness and open our eyes to Jesus's blessed presence. Just as with Elijah, who heard not from earthshaking events but from the still small voice of God, we too will hear God's voice when his Holy Spirit quickens (makes alive) his Word of truth concerning the presence of his dear Son.

In Luke 24:31–32, we read, "Then their eyes were opened and they knew Him; and He vanished from their sight. And they said to one another, did not our hearts burn within us while He talked with us on the road and while *He opened the Scriptures to us?*" (emphasis mine).

We have the same Scriptures plus the New Testament today, and we also have the Holy Spirit within us, who delights in revealing Jesus. John 16 relates Jesus's description of the work of the Holy Spirit, who would be sent to comfort the followers of Christ after he returned to the Father. This will be discussed later, but for now, let us look at John 16:7, in which Jesus says to the disciples, "Nevertheless I tell you the truth. It is to your advantage that I go away; for if I do not go away, the Helper will not come to you; but if I depart, I will send Him to you." To the disciples, this must have come as a shock. This was Jesus talking, the One who had awed them with his power and wisdom for three years. This was the same One they had witnessed performing great miracles, even to the raising of the dead. They had heard his teachings, and from every particle of evidence that had been gained over a three-year period, they had every reason to believe that he was the Son of God. Now, he was talking of one who was to come, whose presence would be an expedient for them. Jesus could not have made them understand that the Holy Spirit would be able to actually live within them—this made possible by what he would accomplish on the cross. Any believer now has within himself or herself the Holy Spirit of the living God. In the capable hands of the Holy Spirit, the remarkable living Word of God does, in truth, become a sword with the capacity to defeat the Enemy and to draw us into a relationship with Jesus and the Father. If we make the Word accessible to the Holy Spirit within us, he will effect changes in our lives. We will no longer walk our Emmaus road, unaware of his presence with us.

As an example, let us consider a problem that has become prominent in our society. Many may be affected by *loneliness*, and it certainly can be one of the most depressing and difficult issues we have to face. I declare God's Word to be the truth; therefore, when it promises that Jesus is with us, I believe that Jesus is with us. Faith in this reality comes about in this manner. First, we receive the Word of God on this particular subject. We could use any Scripture, but for the purposes of our discussion, I have chosen Hebrews 13:5, which reads, "For He Himself has said, I will never leave you nor forsake you." I have chosen a Scripture that, if true, solves the problem, for if we experience the loving presence of Jesus with us, there will be no reason to feel loneliness. This is a clear statement of God's determination to remain with us always and in all circumstances. It is true today, just as it was true for the travelers who walked along the Emmaus road. Let us not forget that it is at this point that Satan will attempt to take away the Word, so that our effort to begin a personal relationship with Jesus will die before it can take root. This is why we must realize that this chosen Scripture is now in the hands of the Holy Spirit within us, a fact made true because we have made the choice to believe his Word. This Word that we have chosen has become the sword of the Spirit, so every time the Evil One comes against us by causing us to think defeatist thoughts, we speak this Word, just like Jesus used the Scripture in the wilderness. Satan will flee from the sword of the Spirit when we use it, just as he was forced to flee when Jesus used it. This is because the Word of God, as a sword, is employed through the powerful Holy Spirit of Christ within us. Not only will Satan depart, but faith in the presence of Jesus will grow as we continue to speak the Word. Remember Romans 10:17—"So then faith comes by hearing, and hearing by the word of God."

To add stimulus for the growth of faith, let us also remember Galatians 5:6, which relates to us that faith works by *love*. As we begin to stand in faith for the presence of Jesus, his love will become reality to the starved soul, and this will further increase our faith. We should add, of course, more and more Scripture verses to our arsenal as we go along. It is true that, at first, we require a certain amount of determination, but it becomes easier as we persist in standing in God's Word of truth. Jesus will be revealed to us, even as he was to those who were on the road to Emmaus.

Let us note that the revelation of Jesus to those who traveled to Emmaus came shortly after his death and, of course, prior to the coming of the Holy Spirit. The Holy Spirit fell upon the early church fifty days later at the feast of Pentecost. Today, we have the advantage of the Holy Spirit within us, whose purpose is to teach us. We now have the Holy Spirit of truth within us (1 Corinthians 3:16), and we have the sword of the Spirit, the Word of God. All we need is a resolution to apply the *truth*, contained in his Word, to the problem, whatever the problem may be.

Even though it may sometimes seem like Satan possesses an indestructible stronghold within our minds—whether loneliness or some other problem—remember that he is the Father of Lies, and our minds have been affected by him throughout each of our lives. Any feeling of being overwhelmed by any problem is a lie, for nothing is impossible with God. That individual who sets his or her face to seek the loving presence of God cannot fail in the endeavor. May we hear what our heavenly Father has to say about the outcome of such an undertaking. Psalm 91:14–16 reads, "Because he has set his love upon Me, therefore I will deliver him; I will set him on high, because he has known My name. He shall call upon Me, and I will answer him, I will be with him in trouble; I will deliver him and honor him. With long life I will satisfy him, and show him my salvation."

Our prayer should be, "Lord, lead us through your Word of truth with the help of your Spirit to behold your presence in every endeavor of life. Let not a moment pass, Lord, in which we do not realize your loving companionship."

Let us place great store in the truth of God's Word, even as he does. Let us realize its absolute perfection and its power and effectiveness as our sword of truth. God, speaking through Isaiah, tells us, "For as the rain cometh down and the snow from heaven and returns not thither; but watereth the earth and makeeth it bring forth and bud, that it may give seed to the sower and bread to the eater: so shall *my word* be that goeth forth out of my mouth: it shall not return unto me void, but it shall accomplish that which I please, and it shall prosper in the thing whereto I sent it" (Isaiah 55:10–11 KJV, emphasis mine).

Joshua was instructed as to how to be successful in leading the children of Israel into the Promised Land. In Joshua 1:8, we read, "This Book of the Law [the Pentateuch—the first five books of the Old Testament as given by Moses, the only Scripture given prior to entrance into the Promised Land] shall not depart from your mouth, but you shall meditate in it day and night, that you may observe to do according to all that is written in it. For then you will make your way prosperous, and then you will have good success." This message that we just read in the book of Joshua is repeated in the first psalm and also speaks of prosperity for the one who delights in the Word of God. We are no longer limited to the Pentateuch but possess the entire Bible, including the Old and New Testaments as our storehouse of truth.

Proverbs 4:20–22 relates, "My son, give attention to my words; incline your ear to my sayings. Do not let them depart from your eyes; keep them in the midst of your heart; for they are life to those who find them, and health to all their flesh."

Jeremiah 15:16 reads, "Your words were found, and I ate them, and Your word was to me the joy and rejoicing of my heart; for I am called by Your name, O Lord God of hosts."

In Numbers 23:19, we read, "God is not a man, that He should lie, nor a son of man, that He should repent. Has He said, and will He not do? Or has He spoken, and will He not make it good?"

In summary, Jesus, by taking unto himself all the sins of lying, cheating, fraudulence, and all forms of deception, delivered humankind from the bondage of satanic deception. Second Corinthians 5:21 tells us," For He made Him who knew no sin (Jesus) to be sin for us." In other words, Jesus laid down his life of sinless truth and became sin in order that we might take up the sword of truth. Allowing his hand to be nailed to the cross, he laid down his sword of truth, which he had wielded so effectively during his ministry on this earth. Paul instructed us in Ephesians 6:17 to take up this great sword of truth (the Word of God). And in John 8:31–32, 36, Jesus said to his disciples, "If you abide in my *word*, then you are my disciples indeed; and you shall know the truth, and the truth shall make you free. ... therefore if the Son makes you free, you shall be free indeed,"

We take up our crosses by refusing to be deceived any further by Satan, who has previously controlled us by prompting us to walk in the flesh, as though our fight was with flesh and blood. Once we have accepted that the battle is, in truth, spiritual, we then realize the insufficiency of carnal weaponry. When we determine to take up our crosses, we must lay down our fleshly weapons, our personal defense mechanisms, and take up the sword of the Spirit, which is the Word of God.

Oh, Father in heaven, deliver us from our preconceived notions concerning self-protection. Help us to learn to rely on you, Jehovah Nissi, our banner, our protector. May we come to know your constant presence with us at all times and come to rest in the spiritual victory you have provided for us. In Jesus's name, we ask it. Amen.

CHAPTER 7

THE SHOES

John answered, saying unto them all,
I indeed baptize you with water,
but one mightier than I cometh,
the latchet of whose shoes
I am not worthy to unloose …

—Luke 3:16

As part of our preparation for the Christian life, Paul instructs the believer to be shod with the preparation of the gospel of peace (Ephesians 6:15). This piece of the believer's attire is vital to a successful Christian walk, even as correct footwear was to a soldier of Paul's day. The great apostle would have the follower of Christ dressed in the armor of a soldier, and the infantry of Paul's day traveled on foot.

In order to place their troops in position for greatest effectiveness in battle, commanders were forced to rely upon the march. Military strategy depended on an army's ability to bring to bear superior numbers upon an enemy's weaknesses, even as it does today. For a soldier to be in perfect position but without his weapon would have rendered him virtually useless. At the same time, he was just as ineffective when out of position, though armed with the finest weaponry. Commanders had to place great importance upon the condition of their troop's footwear.

Our heavenly captain, possessing infinitely greater wisdom than that of any earthly leader, directs us, through the apostle Paul, to be shod with the gospel of peace. With his directive in mind, let us return to the cross from which we gain the necessary understanding and power to do that which he instructs.

A brief refresher is in order so that we may reacquaint ourselves with the previous description of a Roman crucifixion. Each hand was nailed to a crossbeam, which was then attached to an upright beam. The feet were then affixed, one upon the other, to the upright beam by a single nail, which passed through both feet. Obviously, to attach his feet to the cross, the Roman executioners would have had to remove Jesus's shoes. We must always keep in mind that Jesus was not forced to give up his shoes or to have his feet nailed to the cross. Just as he willingly wore the crown of thorns, allowing himself to be beaten, and having permitted his executioners to nail his hands to the cross, the Lamb of God voluntarily bore the nail in his feet. Just as he had sacrificed his heavenly crown, his robe, his shield of faith, and his sword of truth, he sacrificed his shoes, making the way possible for us to have our feet shod with the preparation of the gospel of peace.

Those shoes, removed by his executioners, had been worn by the Prince of Peace as he quieted the storm. They had been made wet when he walked on the waters of the Sea of Galilee. They most likely were covered with dust as he rose to feed the five thousand. Those shoes had borne him to Bethany and to the tomb of Lazarus. Wherever those shoes went, they always left peace in the wake of their passing, for any who would receive it by faith. The One who wore those shoes had fulfilled the prophecy of the angels present at his birth: "peace on earth, goodwill toward men" (Luke 2:14). He truly was the Prince of Peace, and all of those who chose to receive his truth knew it. But henceforth, he would have no need for the shoes that he had used in his mission to bring peace on earth; in the future, he would walk in the shoes of those who would come to believe in him.

He sacrificed his shoes so that all of the thousands who would hear and believe his voice might be shod with his shoes of peace. Jesus dwells within each of us who have received him (John 17:23), and he bids us to allow him to carry his peace through us.

In John 14:27, Jesus said, "Peace I leave with you, my peace I give to you; not as the world gives do I give to you. Let not your heart be troubled, neither let it be afraid." Herein he clearly differentiates between the peace he gives and the peace the world offers. *Webster's Dictionary* defines peace as "the normal, non-warring condition of a nation, group of nations, or the world." In addition, and on a more personal level, a second definition reads "a state of mutual harmony between people or groups of people, especially in personal relations." A third defines peace as "a state or condition conducive to, proceeding from, or characterized by tranquility."

It is indeed obvious that the peace given by the world is that of absence of war on the national level and absence of strife or turmoil on the more personal level. It seems highly unlikely, in light of the past six thousand years, most of which were characterized by war, that the world will ever come to realize this peace spoken of in Mr. Webster's dictionary. On the international scene, we have failed. Following World War I, the attempt to bring about peace through the League of Nations proved fruitless, and subsequently, efforts toward the same end through the United Nations have been no more effective.

Here in the United States, the land of the free, many of our people, in an attempt to find peace, have rejected all limitations in their efforts. It seems as though the more effort that is made, the less peace is found. We are continuously bombarded by the trials and cares of living in this world. Bills for items such as repairs, medicines, and food not only continue to pile up but are each continuously on the increase. The media continues to warn us of this or that illness that threatens to wipe out large portions of the population. Then there is the great threat of terrorism—we may be stricken at any moment by nuclear weapons, conventional explosives, biological weapons, or chemical weapons. Our infrastructure might be attacked, and even if it is not, we are told that much of it could crumble at any time. Our economy is continually threatened. We are informed almost daily of devastating earthquakes, tidal waves, hurricanes, ravaging tornadoes, or massive fires that consume thousands of acres of forest and threaten the lives of large numbers of our fellow citizens.

In view of the present state of affairs on this planet, it is more likely that we will see elephants fly before we experience any peace that this world system has to offer.

But what of the peace that Jesus offers? Philippians 4:6–7 reads, "Be anxious for nothing, but in everything by prayer and supplication, with thanksgiving, let your requests be made known to God; *and the peace of God, which surpasses all understanding,* will guard your hearts and minds through Christ Jesus" (emphasis mine). This peace surpassing understanding does not depend upon *Webster's* peace, which requires the absence of strife. God's peace is peace in the middle of turmoil and stress. Walking peacefully through a situation abounding with trouble obviously requires divine intervention and clearly defies human understanding.

In summary, to have peace when there is nothing present to disturb is to possess the peace of this world, which is, at best, short-lived and temporary. To have peace when everything around is designed to threaten the weary soul is to know the peace of God.

The peace given to us by God comes through the blood that was shed by his Son at Calvary. It results from faith that we are washed in the precious blood of the Lamb and faith that his blood has opened the way to the Father's presence for us. In addition, the peace of God that passes all understanding is a spiritual phenomenon that automatically results from trusting that the Holy Spirit of Christ dwells within us and that the shoes we wear have become his.

This, then, truly is the gospel of peace. We have been fortunate enough to have known or by some means have been made aware of those special people who have exhibited the peace that passes understanding. Those dear souls, in the midst of great tribulation, demonstrated divine serenity. The early church abounded with men and women who sang to their deaths, even as they were subjected to the mouths of wild beasts, having, by their actions, given evidence of the reality of divine peace and having established a precedent for the church to follow.

Most of us know little of the hardships the early church faced, but we are confronted with enough trouble that our lives can serve to contrast the peace of God with the peace of this world. In order to accomplish this state of peace that passes understanding in our own lives, however, we must set about to establish peace between ourselves and God. This peace was made available to us and is simply obtained through faith in the accomplishments of his Son at the cross, but we must receive it. The first step we must take in order to establish true spiritual peace is to renounce all our efforts to make ourselves peaceful.

For many years, I equated peace with happiness, and I set about to find it. I saw the pursuit of happiness as an inalienable right afforded to me by the founders of this nation. I must admit that I worked feverishly toward this elusive "happiness," but, inevitably, it always seemed just around the corner or over the next fence. Several years after I came to know the Lord, I learned that peace and happiness were two different entities. Happiness originates from favorable circumstances. Peace originates from within. This is why peace can exist even in the midst of turbulent circumstances, and happiness cannot.

For this reason, it is absolutely imperative that we determine to reject any attempt to manufacture peace through self-effort. Attempting to fabricate positive circumstances may lead to temporary happiness, but this approach will never create true peace. We must convince ourselves that we will never find that tranquil island that promises peace through solitude. We will not have that jackpot that promises peace through financial gain, even if we are able to accumulate vast wealth (the deceit of riches). We will never gain peace through social relationships; we must bring peace with us to the alliance. Of course, we may experience brief episodes of happiness and pseudo-peace through any or all of the above, including chemical ingestion and altered mental states, but we will not know sustained peace. Nothing on this planet will provide enduring peace, for it can be found only in that which the Prince of Peace has made available. We can be certain that nothing of the self will do! Jesus said in John 15:5, "I am the vine, you are the branches. He who abides in me, and I in him, bears much fruit; *for without me you can do nothing*" (emphasis mine). Do not let the word *fruit* throw you. He is speaking of the fruits of the Spirit, which are "Love, joy, *peace*, patience, gentleness, goodness, faith, meekness, and self-control" (emphasis mine), as recorded in Galatians 5:22–23. There is no way around it; true peace is born of the Spirit, bringing about the truth of the Word of God in us and not of carnal self-effort. Therefore, it should be patently obvious that we must first negotiate a peace with God before attempting to have peace in this carnal world.

Though it may have been short-lived, most Christians who have experienced the love of the Father have walked in his peace at one time or another; as a consequence, you know the peace of which I speak. If that peace eludes you now, determine to return to the cross. As the old hymn goes, "Kneel at the cross; Christ will meet you there. Come while he waits for you. List to his voice; leave with him your care, and begin life anew." As old-fashioned as it may sound to some, there is "power in the blood" that not only offers salvation for eternity and victory over the Evil One but also the triumph of walking in "the peace that passes all understanding." Ephesians 2:13 reads, "But now in Christ Jesus you who once were far off have been brought near by the *blood of Christ*" (emphasis mine). There is unquestionably no way to find peace with almighty God except through his Son and, more specifically, through the blood of his Son, which was shed at Calvary.

In order for the children of Israel to be at peace with God, the Creator established a "peace offering." These were special sacrificial offerings designed by God to create peace and fellowship between him and humankind. God presented Moses with specific, detailed instructions as to how the offering was to be presented. He even went so far as to place restrictions concerning the altar stones upon which the offering was to be sacrificed. Exodus 20:24–25 reads, "An altar of earth you shall make for Me, and you shall sacrifice on it your burnt offerings and your *peace offerings,* your sheep and your oxen. In every place where I record My name I will come to you and I will bless you and if you make Me an altar of stone, you shall not build it of hewn stone; *for if you use your tool on it, you have profaned it*" (emphasis mine).

This peace between the Creator and his creation, which is greatly desired by the Almighty, is extremely important to both parties. Therefore, the means to arrive at this coveted objective had to be divinely accomplished without any input on the part of humankind, except that of humble acceptance. Any stone disturbed by human effort was automatically rejected by God, just as any human effort to create peace between God and man is destined to be rejected. Just as carnal handiwork upon the stones would have polluted the sacrifice, human effort will also pollute the acquisition of peace. The "peace that passes understanding" will never be obtained through any combination of divine and fleshly achievement; only the work of the Father through his Son will do.

This peace offering was second only to the burnt offering made for the atonement of sins. The burnt offering made it possible for a person to come to God in worship. The blood of the perfect Lamb (Jesus) fulfilled this requirement as far as we are concerned. Hebrews 9:19–22 reads, "For when Moses had spoken every precept to all the people according to the law, he took the blood of calves and goats, with water, scarlet wool, and hyssop, and sprinkled both the book itself and all the people, saying,, 'this is the blood of the covenant which God has commanded you.' Then likewise he sprinkled with blood both the tabernacle and all the vessels of the ministry. And according to the law almost all things are purified with blood, and without shedding of blood there is no remission."

To anyone who finds repulsive this talk of shedding of blood and is therefore inclined to seek some other means of redemption, be certain that none will be found. Hebrews 9:11–12 tells us, "But Christ came as High Priest of the good things to come, with the greater and more perfect tabernacle not made with hands, that is, not of this creation. Not with the blood of goats and calves, *but with His own blood He entered the Most Holy Place once for all, having ordained eternal redemption*" (emphasis mine). This phrase in the King James translation reads, "...by his own blood he entered in once into the holy place, having obtained eternal redemption *for us*" (emphasis mine). *Just as redemption is obtained through the blood of Christ, so is peace.* The peace offering firmly established, before God, the worshiper's desire to be at peace with his Creator. That sacrifice, when performed properly, made that peace possible.

In Jesus, the *final blood sacrifice was accomplished*. No longer would animals be sacrificed, for within Christ and his cross, all was accomplished. His blood was sufficient to atone for the sins of all humankind and to establish peace between the Creator and his creation for all eternity. There would never be a need for humankind to sacrifice a peace offering again. Humanity's only obligation in the matter is simple trust in what the Father has spoken through his Word. Peace is wholly available through faith in the blood of Jesus.

Now let us return to Ephesians 2:13, which reads, "But now in Christ Jesus, you who once were [so] far away, through (by, in) the blood of Christ have been brought near" (AB). It is here in this nearness to the Father, the Son, and the Holy Spirit that peace abides. All things have been reconciled through the blood of Jesus unto himself. Oh, the power of the blood of Jesus that made it possible for every person who ever lived on the face of this earth to be reconciled, in Christ, to God. One of my favorite Scriptures is found in Colossians 1:19–20, which reads, "For it pleased the Father

117

that in him [Jesus] should all fullness dwell; and, *having made peace through the blood of the cross*, by him to reconcile all things unto himself; by him, I say, whether they be things in earth, or things in heaven" (KJV, emphasis mine).

As mentioned earlier, peace is almost nonexistent in the United States of America and, indeed, in the world as a whole, because peace in the eyes of the world can only be manufactured by humanity. Many Christians seek peace in the same manner. But there is a third category—and possibly a more pitiable one—composed of those who go to God in prayer, sincerely pleading for God-given peace, not realizing that Jesus is peace. It is in him that peace is found. To reject Jesus is to reject peace. But it is also true that if we ask for peace apart from his presence, it is a little bit like asking him to go to the bucket of peace and pour us out a cupful. This really does not work either, for in perfect truth, peace goes where he goes. A relatively unknown verse of Scripture sums it up: *"Now the Lord of peace himself give you peace always by all means. The Lord be with you all"* (2 Thessalonians 3:16 KJV, emphasis mine), inferring that the presence of Jesus is the means by which we will know his peace.

It seems rational that if we desire peace, we should seek him, who is peace. Instead of looking for the gift of peace, we would be far better off to seek the giver of the peace. To do otherwise is a little like being in a dark room, wishing for light, when located in the next room is a wonderful source of light. All I have to do is to move near the light to have it. The same is true where peace is concerned; we have only to move close to Jesus to have it.

In order to obtain and maintain a close relationship with Christ, we simply follow the principles already outlined in previous chapters. We stand on the truth of God's Word, refusing to allow Satan to tempt us into doubting God's Word. If Jesus had not desired that those who believe in him should have peace, he never would have said, "Peace I give unto you." So as previously discussed, we believe the words of God over our minds, emotions, or any temptation of the Evil One. To do this, we must build our faith by reading, memorizing, quoting, and—through every possible means—hearing the Word of God on the subject of the presence of Christ in our lives.

We begin by asserting our determination to keep the presence of the Lord fresh in our minds. He will hear, and he will respond to our desires. This is so true—when he detects one of God's children attempting to draw near to him, he will draw near to that child of God, even as a mother draws near to her crying child. Psalm 145:18–19 reads, "The Lord is nigh unto all them that call upon him, to all that call upon him in truth. He will fulfill the desire of them that fear him: he also will hear their cry, and will save them" (KJV). Through his mercy, we may receive other things that we need, but when our desires place him at the forefront of our searches, we will never be disappointed. I like what the Lord said about this in the messianic prophecy found in Jeremiah 31:31-34.

> Behold, the days are coming, says the Lord, when I will make a new covenant with the house of Israel and with the house of Judah—not according to the covenant that I made with their fathers in the day that I took them by the hand to lead them out of the land of Egypt, My covenant which they broke, though I was a husband to them, says the Lord. But this is the covenant that I will make with the house of Israel after those days, says the Lord: I will put My law in their minds, and write it on their hearts; and I will be their God and they shall be My people. No more shall every man teach his neighbor, and every man his brother, saying, *'know the Lord' for they all shall know Me,* from the least of them to the greatest of them, says the Lord, for I will forgive their iniquity, and their sin I will remember no more." (emphasis mine)

Isaiah 26:3 reads, *"You will keep him in perfect peace, whose mind is stayed on You*, because he trusts in You" (emphasis mine). Again, we see here a distinct connection between having our minds set on him and his presence and that peace that results from having done so. We need to seek the Lord and make this the main priority in our lives. One of the most interesting portions of Scripture is found in 2 Chronicles 15. Verse 1 begins, "Now the Spirit of God came upon Azariah the son of Oded. And he went out to meet Asa [King of Judah], and said to him: hear me, Asa, and all Judah and Benjamin. The Lord is with you while you are with Him. If you seek Him, He will be found by you; but if you forsake Him, He will forsake you." Upon hearing the prophecy of Azariah, the Bible says that Asa "... took courage, and he removed the abominable idols from all the land of Judah and Benjamin and from the cities which he had taken in the mountains of Ephraim; and he restored the altar of the Lord that was before the vestibule of the Lord" (2 Chronicles 15:8). Asa then gathered together at Jerusalem all Judah and Benjamin and many of the people of Ephraim, Manasseh, and Simeon. We pick up the text at 2 Chronicles 15:11–15.

> And they offered to the Lord at that time seven hundred bulls and seven thousand sheep from the spoil they had brought. Then they entered into a covenant to seek the Lord God of their fathers with all their heart and with all their soul; and *whosoever would not seek the Lord God of Israel was to be put to death*, whether small or great, whether man or woman. Then they took an oath before the Lord with a loud voice, with shouting and trumpets and ram's horns. And all Judah rejoiced at the oath, for they had sworn with all their heart and sought Him with all their soul; and He was found by them, and the Lord gave them rest all around. (emphasis mine)

The Amplified Bible reads, "And the Lord gave them *rest and peace* round about" (emphasis mine).

These people of Judah were of one accord in their determination to seek the Lord. Their seriousness in this endeavor could never be questioned, as anyone who refused would have been put to death. Oh, that our great country could have a leader or leaders who would seriously call this nation to seek God with all its heart. It is extremely unlikely that the USA, as a whole, will ever admit its need for God, much less make a covenant to seek him, but at the individual level, each of us has this opportunity; all we have to do is to supply the will to see it done. If we are to have peace, we must seek the God of peace. David said in Psalm 27:4, "One thing have I desired of the Lord, that will I seek: that I may dwell in the house of the Lord all the days of my life, to behold the beauty of the Lord, and to inquire in His temple." And in Psalm 42:1, we read, "As the deer pants for the water brooks, so pants my soul for You, O God." Moses sought God's presence:

> Then Moses said to the Lord, see, You say to me, 'bring up this people.' But You have not let me know whom You will send with me. Yet You have said, 'I know you by name and you have also found grace in My sight.' Now therefore, I pray, if I have found grace in Your sight, show me now Your way, that I may know You and that I may find grace in Your sight. And consider that this nation is Your people. And He [God] said, *My presence will go with you* and I will give you rest. Then he [Moses] said to Him, *if Your presence does not go with us, do not bring us up from here.* (Exodus 33:12–15, emphasis mine)

Great leaders, whose deeds are recorded in the Holy Scriptures, were very acquainted with the need for the presence of God. Long before he led the triumphant children of Israel in taking the Promised

Land, Joshua was noted to have remained in the tabernacle *in the presence of God*, even after Moses had departed (Exodus 33:11). The writer of Psalm 43 pleads with the Lord in verse 3, "Oh, send out Your light and Your truth! Let them lead me; let them bring me to Your holy hill and to your tabernacle."

The above-mentioned were all great men of God, but what does the Scripture say about those of us who hold no such exalted position before God? No matter what our status may be, God desires that we seek him. Hebrews 11:6 tells us that God "...is a rewarder of them that diligently seek Him." Psalm 105:4 implores us: "Seek the Lord and His strength; seek His face evermore!" And in Isaiah 55:6, he exhorts us to "Seek the Lord while He may be found, call upon Him while He is near."

Hebrews 11:6 has informed us that God is a rewarder of them that diligently seek him, but what are the rewards? Let us look at the Amplified Bible's rendering of 2 Chronicles 15:15, "And all Judah rejoiced at the oath, for they had sworn with all their heart and sought him [yearning for him] with their whole desire, and he was found by them. And the Lord gave them rest and peace round about." Psalm 16:11 reads, "You will show me the path of life; *in Your presence is fullness of joy, at Your right hand there are pleasures forevermore*" (AB, emphasis mine). And in Hosea 10:12, we read, "Sow to yourselves in righteousness [uprightness and right standing with God]; reap in mercy: break up your fallow ground: for it is time to seek the Lord, till he come and rain righteousness upon you" (KJV).

So we see that in 2 Chronicles 15:15, we receive peace; in Psalm 16:11, we find joy in his presence; and in Hosea 10:12, we are given the gift of righteousness. Romans 14:17 defines the kingdom of God as "righteousness, peace, and joy in the Holy Ghost." So in seeking God, we are simultaneously seeking the kingdom of God. Carrying this thought a step further, let us look at what Jesus said about the results of seeking God's kingdom: "Therefore do not worry, saying, 'What shall we eat?' Or 'What shall we drink?' Or 'What shall we wear?' For after all these things the Gentiles seek. For your heavenly Father knows that you need all these things. But seek first the kingdom of God and His righteousness, and all these things shall be added unto you" (Matthew 6:31–33).

To sum up, we can say that in seeking the Lord, the end result is that we not only find him, but we also find in him everything that we need to live in his kingdom and all the necessities required for life in this world.

We can see, then, that the kingdom of God is "righteousness and peace and joy in the Holy Spirit" (Romans 14:17); therefore, peace is an integral part of the kingdom of God and cannot be separated from it.

We know that Jesus at the cross made it possible for us to have our feet shod with the preparation of the gospel of peace. We know that his Spirit dwells within each believer; therefore, our shoes became his shoes at the moment when the Holy Spirit took up residence within each of us. His shoes, in the natural, will never walk the dusty roads of Judea or Galilee ever again; they were removed by the Roman soldiers in preparation for his crucifixion. He now bids us to awaken to the fact that he desires to carry his gospel of peace to this lost and dying world by wearing our shoes.

By taking up our cross to follow Jesus, we surrender our carnal shoes, thereby allowing our feet to be shod with the gospel of peace. By denying ourselves the pursuit of the peace offered by this world, we are left with that peace that Jesus provided.

Abba Father, we humbly beseech you to help us to remove these carnal shoes that have carried us, at our own bidding, these many years. May we learn, dear Father, to submit our wills and surrender our feet to be shod with the gospel of peace, that your peace might be spread far and wide over this belligerent world in which we live. In Jesus's name, we ask it. Amen.

CHAPTER 8

THE BREASTPLATE

For he put on righteousness as a breastplate
and an helmet of salvation upon his head ...
—Isaiah 59:17

We have now reached the seventh and final anatomical site from which blood flowed from the body of Christ. In order to prevent the bodies of Jesus and the two thieves from remaining on the cross on the Sabbath, the Jewish leadership appealed to Pilate to order the legs of the crucified broken in order to expedite their deaths. The legs of the thieves were then broken, assuring accelerated death by suffocation. However, John 19:33, tells us, "...when they came to Jesus and saw that He was already dead, they did not break His legs." It is of note that in their reluctance to break Jesus's legs, they unknowingly fulfilled the prophecy of Psalm 34:20, which reads, "He guards all his bones; not one of them is broken." John 19:34 continues, "But one of the soldiers pierced His side with a spear, and immediately blood and water came out."

This was irrefutable evidence in the eyes of his executioners that Jesus had ceased to live. The erythrocytes (red blood cells) and the serum had separated, indicating that blood had ceased to flow through the vascular system. This, the final portal, heralded Jesus's demise. It is highly likely that the spear penetrated the heart of Jesus, for Roman soldiers were expertly trained and, therefore, skilled in administering the death blow. And the introduction of the spear into the heart would have absolutely assured them of the death of Jesus, even if he had not expired before.

As the sacrificial lamb of the Passover had died that day for the sins of Israel, Jesus had died that day for the sins of the whole world for all eternity. As the Passover lamb had taken on the sins of Israel's children for one year, the true Lamb had taken upon himself the sins of humankind from Adam to the last person to live on the face of this earth. Hebrews 10:12–13 reads, "But this man, after He had offered one sacrifice for sins forever, sat down at the right hand of God, from that time waiting till His enemies are made His footstool."

To emphasize the need for the believer to return to the cross and review what our Lord did there, I will repeat a relevant fact that easily might be overlooked. On the day of Christ's crucifixion, the chief priest sacrificed the Passover lamb in accordance with the Law that had been handed down from Moses. At the same time, the real Lamb of God was being sacrificed, establishing an entirely new covenant based upon the grace and mercy of almighty God. God was, at that very moment, opening the gates of heaven to those who would believe that the blood of his Son justified them in his sight. John 1:17 reads, "For the law [the old covenant that required animal sacrifice] was given through Moses, but grace and truth [the new covenant that required the sacrifice of the Son of God] came through Jesus Christ."

Prior to the sacrifice of the Passover lamb, the priest was obligated to ensure the perfection of the lamb selected for the sacrifice. On this particular Passover, this priest must have performed according to custom, ensuring the perfection of the Passover lamb of the old covenant. On the previous night, that same priest had examined (judged) the Lamb of the new covenant (Jesus) and found him unworthy. This Lamb, who had been approved by almighty God in heaven as the sacrifice for all the sins of humankind (including, by the way, those committed by the high priest), was judged worthy only of crucifixion—a blasphemer who merited only the vilest treatment. Steeped in the trappings of his religious orthodoxy, the high priest must have believed that he held a favorable position with God, even as he passed the sentence of death upon the Son of God. In his attempt to preserve the religious status quo, he placed himself at cross purposes with God. The fundamental truth is summed up in the fact that the priest judged not only the Lamb of God but God himself (Jesus), who would die on the cross, the result of a sentence handed down by a misguided priest. The question begs to be asked: how could this man, while looking directly into the eyes of God as he judged Jesus, have determined that he [Jesus] was not worthy to be the Lamb of God who would take away the sin of the world? A right relationship with Jehovah would have almost certainly assured him that he was actually looking into the eyes of God. While he should have been on his knees before Jesus, pleading for his life, he was, instead, judging the very One who held the keys of life and death in his hand. The Bible says that whosoever believes in him shall not perish but have everlasting life (John 3:16). That word *whosoever* included Caiaphas, the high priest. He could have opened his heart to Jesus and gained eternal fellowship with the God that he supposedly served, but instead he ignored the true plan of God, clinging to the cold hard religion to which he was enslaved, and forfeited his right to the New Covenant in Christ.

We cannot allow ourselves any longer to remain blinded by the cold, unfeeling ritual formality of religion. We must position ourselves beneath the cross in order to feed upon the passion of our Lord. We must come to the point where we sense his willingness to endure the horrors of the cross in order to establish a living, vibrant relationship with each of us. We must begin to make ourselves available to receive his love for us. He does not seek to tie us down to a tyrannical religion composed of dos and don'ts; he desires a relationship of love that binds us to his heart.

unachievable goal that produced feelings of guilt and condemnation. As soon as trouble came into my life, my mind automatically blamed the situation on my lack of righteousness (my inability to maintain my part of the bargain with God). I found myself almost continuously straddled with feelings of condemnation—that is, until I realized that true freedom to walk in peace with God is found in an understanding of God's righteousness. This is true because righteousness was made available through the blood of his dear Son, and it has never been dependent upon my behavior. God, by his grace, sees us through the blood of his Son, and we can come to him by exercising faith in the sacrifice made by Jesus on the cross.

Webster's Dictionary defines righteousness as "(1) Characterized by uprightness or morality: a righteous observance of the law; (2) Morally right or justifiable; (3) Acting in a moral upright way." Then there is the typical definition, which was and is heard from many pulpits: "right standing with God." For several years of my Christian life, I was caught up in something of a dilemma. I firmly believed that Jesus saved me by the grace of God, but I was left to work out *Webster's* definition of righteousness on my own. I truly desired that relationship with God that I heard others talk about and that I found in books and in the Bible. I experimented with one formula after another without success. I would perform fairly well at times, but the inevitable fall would always come, and in despair, I would give up, having failed to maintain standards I had set for myself. It was a life of ups and downs, mountaintops and valleys. Even on the mountain, there were many times underlying feelings of dread, for I knew that I would, most probably, return to the valley. There was never the security that I seriously desired in a loving relationship with the One who never changes. And it seemed at the time as though I would never find that close association with the Lord because I would never be able to fulfill the dictionary definition: "a righteous observance of the law." For a long time, I attempted to maintain a righteous appearance by doing those things other men seemed to consider acceptable, but I knew that this standard was far below a "righteous observance of the law." I passed the test when I graded myself by the curve of man's opinion, but in doing so, I never found that place I longed for—that nearness to the heart of God.

I was fortunate in that several years ago, the Holy Spirit placed me in a position to hear a sermon that emphasized 2 Corinthians 5:21. I already understood that righteousness somehow equated to being near God. I guess this was because I had heard the words "right standing with God" so many times. With this in mind, the words "we have been made righteous" stood out from that verse in 2 Corinthians like a neon sign. I began to study the Scripture pertaining to righteousness and found confirmation that faith in the complete work of Jesus on the cross made me righteous before God. It was not something for which I had to strive. My only responsibility was to believe in the completeness of what Jesus already had accomplished. Just as I had believed in Jesus's accomplishment at the cross for my salvation unto eternal life, I had to believe that his work at the cross provided my righteousness, which, in turn, produced a relationship with Father, Son, and Holy Spirit. There was nothing I could do to obtain eternal life except believe in Jesus; just as certainly, there was nothing I could do except believe in Jesus for my righteousness. My only responsibility was to believe in what Jesus had done. It became obvious that this breastplate of righteousness that I had received as a free gift would protect my heart, constantly reminding me of my right standing with a loving and merciful Father.

As mentioned, for all of those years when I could not find the way to righteousness and union with the Lord, I always tended to blame myself for my inability to hold up what I saw as my part of the bargain. I saw Jesus and all that he had accomplished and sincerely thought that he was there to *help me* accomplish my task of becoming righteous. Since I never could see myself as righteous by trying to work it out myself, guilt and condemnation were always the result. However, when I began to see righteousness as a free gift, it was no longer necessary to look at myself and what I had done; I could now focus on Jesus and his shed blood, realizing that he and his blood were all that I would ever need. No longer would condemnation have the upper hand in driving me to despair, for all I had to do was to go before my Father, not run away from him, when I had done wrong.

I could better comprehend what Paul meant in Romans 8:1–3: "Therefore, there is now no condemnation for those who are in Christ Jesus, because through Christ Jesus the law of the Spirit of life set me free from the law of sin and death. For what the law was powerless to do in that it was weakened by the sinful nature [my self-effort to obey the law], God did by sending his own Son in the likeness of sinful man to be a sin offering" (NIV). I would be bound no longer by *Webster's* definition—"righteous observance of the law"—for Jesus had "made me free from the law of sin and death." I was no longer ignorant of the righteousness of God. Romans 10:3–4 refers to ignorance of the righteousness of God; it reads, "For they being ignorant of God's righteousness, and seeking to establish their own righteousness, have not submitted to the righteousness of God. *For Christ is the end of the law for righteousness to everyone who believes*"(emphasis mine). Though it is impossible for a person, Christian or otherwise, to live free from sin, it is no longer possible for that sin to separate us from God. All that is necessary to remain near him is to remain in agreement with him concerning sin. We show our agreement by confessing sin when we commit it and requesting that he cleanse us from it. I simply tell him that I realize that what I have done is wrong, and I don't want to do it, but I know that the old nature in me will continue to do wrong until he, through the blood of Jesus, cleanses me from it (1 John 1:9).

Our breastplate of righteousness must be firmly secured in place if it is to protect as it should. When properly adjusted, it will cause the believer to reign in life over all the efforts of the Enemy. Romans 5:17–21 reads:

> For if by the one man's offense death reigned through
> the one, much more those who receive abundance

of grace and of the gift of *righteousness* will reign in life through the One, Jesus Christ. Therefore, as through one man's offense judgment came to all men, resulting in condemnation, even so *through one Man's righteous act the free gift came to all men, resulting in justification of life.* For as by one man's disobedience many were made sinners, so also by one Man's obedience many will be made righteous. Moreover, the law entered that the offense might abound. But where sin abounded, *grace abounded much more,* so that as sin reigned in death, even so grace might reign through *righteousness* to eternal life through Jesus Christ our Lord. (emphasis mine)

We do not have to construct the breastplate, and we do not have to purchase one; this part of the armor is there for all believers, and all we have to do is to put it on by faith. All attempts to make ourselves righteous through our own efforts will only result in failure. Galatians 5:4–5 reads, "You have become estranged from Christ, you who attempt to be justified by law [your own efforts to fulfill the law]; you have fallen from grace. For we through the Spirit eagerly wait for the hope of righteousness by faith." And in Philippians 3:8–9, we read, "Yet indeed, I also count all things loss for the excellence of the knowledge of Christ Jesus my Lord, for whom I have suffered the loss of all things and count them as rubbish, that I may gain Christ, and be found in him, *not having my own righteousness,* which is from the law [self-effort] but that which is through the faith in Christ, *the righteousness which is from God by faith;...* " (emphasis mine). And in Hebrews 11:7, we read, "By faith Noah, being divinely warned of things not yet seen, moved with godly fear, prepared an ark for the saving of his household, by which he condemned the world and became heir of the *righteousness which is according to faith*" (emphasis mine). Galatians 2:21 reads, "I do not set aside the grace of God; for if *righteousness* comes through the law [self-effort], then Christ died in vain" (emphasis mine). Galatians 3:6 reads, "Just as Abraham believed God, and it was accounted to him for *righteousness*" (emphasis mine). And Galatians 3:11 reads, "But that no one is justified by the law in the sight of God is evident, for the just shall live by faith." The just are those who have been justified in the sight of God by the blood of his Son. The gospel of Jesus Christ is obviously the gospel of justification by faith, and all attempts to make it justification by my self-effort are destined to fail.

We should make this a part of our daily testimony. I received the gift of righteousness by faith in the blood of Jesus Christ, shed for me on the cross, and therefore, I am righteous in the eyes of God through the blood of Jesus Christ. I am deeply loved by my Father, his Son Jesus, and the Holy Spirit because my Father has made me accepted in the beloved, according to Ephesians 1:6.

Remember that righteousness is right standing with God. By making us righteous, Jesus has prepared us to walk with the Father in perfect harmony. In other words, we have been brought back to the original state of Adam before the fall and even beyond that, for *Christ lives within us through his Holy Spirit*. Psalm 23:3–4 tells us, "He leads me in the paths of *righteousness* for his name's sake. Yea, though I walk through the valley of the shadow of death, I will fear no evil; *for You are with me*; your rod and your staff, they comfort me" (emphasis mine). If we accept the definition of righteousness as right standing with God, then we can conclude that David is telling us that God leads in paths that place the believer in right standing or *nearness* to him. Placed in this position near to God, nothing can make him fear. It is this righteousness that made nearness to God possible for David. It is, therefore, the absence of righteousness in the case of the nonbeliever or the erroneous perception of the absence of righteousness in the believer that separates from God. Remember 2 Corinthians 5:21—"For he has made him [Jesus] to be sin for us, who knew no sin; that we might be made the righteousness of God in him" (KJV). We are made righteous through the blood of Jesus that was shed at the cross, and it is through this path of righteousness that we are made near to God. And when we receive by faith this righteousness that has been freely given to us, we too can know the victory of walking without fear "through the valley of the shadow of death," because we will have come to the realization that God is present with us.

God's amazing grace has provided the free gift of righteousness, through faith in his Son, to all who will receive it. No amount of effort on the part of the believer will make him or her either more righteous or less righteous; this righteousness comes through faith that Jesus took our sins upon himself, laying down his breastplate of righteousness so that he could become sin for us. All we must do is put on the breastplate of righteousness, graciously provided for us all by our Savior.

As previously mentioned, Isaiah 53 is a prophetic Scripture that describes the suffering of Jesus on the cross. We read, "Therefore I will divide Him a portion with the great, and He shall divide the spoil with the strong, because He poured out His soul unto death, and *He was numbered with the transgressors, and He bore the sin of many,* and made intercession for the transgressors" (Isaiah 53:12, emphasis mine). If chapter 53 of Isaiah predicts the coming death of the Messiah, chapter 54 outlines the results of what Jesus's death will mean to his followers. We read, *"in righteousness you shall be established*; you shall be far from oppression for *you shall not fear*; and from terror, for it shall not come near you. Indeed they shall surely assemble, but not because of Me. Whoever assembles against you shall fall for your sake" (Isaiah 54:14–15, emphasis mine). As is the case in Psalm 23, righteousness (right standing or nearness to God) renders us capable of walking through any valley without fear. Fear and terror shall gather against the believer, according to Isaiah 54:15, but they shall fall. They fall because the believer is covered by the whole armor of God that is provided through the precious blood of Jesus. Having been washed by the blood of Jesus and wearing his armor, the believer will be victorious.

However, if the Enemy gathers his forces together against the Christian and finds that he or she is dressed in anything but the armor of God, he will most certainly win the battle. For example, let us use the breastplate of righteousness: if the believer is wearing the breastplate of righteousness that has been provided by faith in the gift of righteousness, he wins. On the other hand, if his righteousness is like that of the scribes and Pharisees (that of self-effort, self-righteousness), then he will surely fail. Jesus said in Matthew 5:20, "For I say to you, that unless your righteousness exceeds the righteousness of the scribes and Pharisees, you will by no means enter the kingdom of heaven." Their righteousness was based on their ability to keep the Law. Remember: "Being ignorant of God's righteousness and going about to establish their own righteousness have not submitted themselves unto the righteousness of God. For Christ is the end of the law for righteousness to every one that believeth" (Romans 10:3 KJV).

The adversary will surely come against our newly found freedom in Christ. He certainly does not want any believer to understand that faith in the righteousness provided by Christ is all that God requires for the justification of humankind. If he can keep the believer bound by feeling that he has to keep the Law in order to maintain fellowship with God, then he has that person enslaved. Living in the continual torment that results from fear that an infraction of the Law will cause separation from God serves as a primary yoke for keeping the Christian subservient to the forces of darkness. But Satan is a defeated foe, for Colossians 2:13–14 reads, "And you, being dead in your trespasses and the uncircumcision of your flesh, He has made alive together with Him having forgiven you all trespasses, *having wiped out the handwriting of requirements that was against us*, which was contrary to us. And He has taken it out of the way, having nailed it to the cross" (emphasis mine). The King James Version refers to the "handwriting of requirements" as the "handwriting of ordinances"; an ordinance is a rule of law, and Paul tells us here that the law was nailed to the cross. Does this mean that God has lowered his standards? Does this mean that the law is any less of divine origin? Does this mean that the law is any less demanding? Has God become soft on sin? Of course this is not true! No. No. No. God is the same God who gave the Law to Moses at Mount Sinai. He is like Jesus, who, according to Hebrews 13:8, is "The same yesterday, and today, and forever." His Law, therefore, requires complete obedience to all of its statutes. Failure to keep any single commandment in detail is tantamount to disobedience in all of the Law. James 2:10 reads, "For whosoever shall keep the whole law, and yet offend in one point, he is guilty of all" (KJV).

During his ministry on earth, did Jesus teach that he came to earth in order to somehow make the Law more malleable? No! He said, "And it is easier for heaven and earth to pass, than one tittle of the law to fail" (Luke 16:17 KJV). And in Matthew 5:17–18, he said, "Think not that I am come to destroy the law, or the prophets; I am not come to destroy, but to *fulfill*. For verily I say unto you, till heaven and earth pass, one jot or one tittle shall in no wise pass from the law, till all be fulfilled" (KJV, emphasis mine). He even supercharged the Law, making it even more demanding than it was before he came to this earth. He placed anger on the same level with murder and elevated lust to the same plane with adultery. In Matthew 5:21–22, Jesus said, "Ye have heard that it was said by them of old time, thou shalt not kill; and whosoever shall kill shall be in danger of the judgment: but I say unto you that whosoever is angry with his brother without a cause shall be in danger of the judgment" (KJV). And in Matthew 5:27–28, "You have heard that it was said by them of old time, thou shalt not commit adultery: but I say unto you, that whosoever looketh on a woman to lust after her has committed adultery with her already in his heart" (KJV). Not even a superficial reading of the Bible can give any impression that Jesus came to this world to eradicate the divine Law of almighty God.

The Law is just as demanding as it ever was and requires divine perfection, which is altogether unachievable on the human level. Saddled by a carnal nature with its propensity toward sin and, at the same time, facing an unforgiving law that required death (Romans 6:23) as punishment for any infraction, humankind's state, without Christ, was and is one of hopeless desperation.

It was into this quagmire of desolation that the Son of God came, bearing the good news of redemption. Taking the sin of humankind upon himself, he submitted to the cross. In so doing, he paid the price for all sin, which had been and would ever be committed by anyone who would ever live upon earth. His death, while certainly not eradicating the Law, paid the debt that was owed by *every human*, for Romans 3:23 tells us, "All have sinned and fallen short of the glory of God." Jesus, in his sinless perfection, went to the cross, completing his mission, which was to fulfill the law, according to Matthew 5:17. Looking back now to Colossians 2:14, which says that Jesus blotted out the handwriting of ordinances, or law, and took it out of the way and nailed it to his cross, we can better understand that Jesus did not destroy the Law; instead, he fulfilled the Law. Humankind would no longer be judged by whether or not he or she kept the Law but by whether or not an individual trusted that Jesus's blood was and is sufficient to pay the debt for sin.

God would see any violation of Law through the blood of his Son. The Holy Spirit's presence within the believer assures recognition of wrongdoing on the part of the believer (conviction), and simple acknowledgment, accompanied by sincere desire to be rid of the sin (confession), further assures cleansing from it. First John 1:9 reads, "If we confess our sins, He is faithful and just to forgive us our sins and to cleanse us from all unrighteousness." Not only does the blood of Jesus offer us forgiveness for our sins, but it also assumes the responsibility for cleansing us from them. The only means of possessing power over sin is through the blood of Jesus, the Word of God, and the work of the Holy Spirit within us. Any effort on the part of the individual (self-effort) is not only useless and doomed to failure but is, in actuality, an infraction of the Law of the Spirit. *"For the law of the Spirit of life in Christ Jesus has made me free from the law of sin and death"* (Romans 8:2, emphasis mine).

Human attempts at behavior-pattern correction may frustrate the efforts of the Holy Spirit. I wasted many years in an effort to alter behavior I perceived as inconsistent with the Christian life. I call them wasted years because with all my striving, very little was ever accomplished. I can now praise the Lord for revealing his plan for bringing his children into a victorious and productive life. I have not arrived, but I have made progress and have gained hope for further advancement. This is all because of the divine plan, which allows absolutely no input from us, as human beings, except faith in his ability to bring the one who seeks his presence into the abundant life that Jesus offers. Earlier, we discussed that human enterprise is destined to fail, but I would like to probe the biblical evidence in more depth to better determine God's estimation of it. Let us look back to the children of Israel and their journey after departing Egypt.

Most biblical scholars view the Red Sea crossing by the Israelites as spiritually likened to the salvation experience for the Christian. We discussed how the Promised Land for the children of Israel corresponds spiritually with the abundant life offered by Christ. If we continue the allegory, since the children of Israel experienced battle shortly after their Red Sea crossing, the young Christian would be wise to prepare for spiritual war. This is why it is necessary for the Christian to put on the armor that was provided by Christ at the cross and clearly described by Paul in Ephesians 6.

The children of God witnessed the miraculous division of the Red Sea and the destruction of Pharaoh's army. They were finally free from Egyptian tyranny after four hundred years of captivity—and all this without so much as a skirmish. God had planned and executed their complete salvation without any assistance from them. All the children of Israel were required to do was to follow as God gave them direction through Moses. However, they soon found their progress completely blocked by forces that were determined to see them perish in the wilderness.

The freed slaves of Israel, their feet barely dry from the Red Sea crossing, had pitched in Rephidim when "Then came Amalek and fought with Israel in Rephidim" (Exodus 17:8 KJV).

If we fast-forward forty years, we find the children of those Israelites who had crossed the Red Sea having just crossed the Jordan River into the Promised Land. Just as their forebears faced battle with Amalek, this new generation of Israelites was faced, immediately, with battle at Jericho. So it will be for the new believer in Christ. As we step into this new life, we too will be challenged by the adversary. Unfortunately, far too little is made of the battle that we, as new Christians, will have to face. Hence, we find ourselves surrounded by forces of the Enemy and completely unprepared to withstand their assault. Remember the parable of the sower: "Satan comes immediately to steal the word." He strikes quickly and always at the weakest point in the Christian's armor.

The situation for the children of Israel at Rephidim and that of their descendants at Jericho sounds hauntingly familiar for the would-be soldier in Christ's army. Having been miraculously rescued from the slavery of a life without Christ, we are soon forced into battle in the spiritual realm, and unfortunately, many times we are unprepared. Because of the similarities between Israel's battle with Amalek and Jericho and that with which the Christian is faced, let us attempt to learn from the comparison. Also, we should keep in mind that Jesus, after his baptism, went directly into the wilderness to do battle with Satan. The same vigilance and determination with which the Israelites faced Amalek and Jericho and with which Jesus faced Satan must be employed by the Christian as he or she faces those forces that will certainly attempt to block his or her path toward a victorious Christian life.

What can be gleaned from a study of the response of the children of Israel to these battles they faced? Let us look first at those who faced battle at Jericho. From the natural standpoint, the great walled city should never have fallen to the Israelites. However, with God's intervention, combined with a group of people who were determined to do his absolute bidding, Jericho was destroyed. All animal life was put to death and the city burned. Only the precious metals and the brass and iron were saved, and these were supposed to be deposited into the treasury of the house of the Lord.

We are told that as a result of this great victory over Jericho, all the country 'round about, including the followers of Joshua, knew that the Lord was with Israel. The fame of Joshua spread throughout the land (Joshua 6:27).

This was the Lord's victory. Neither Joshua nor those who followed him should be assigned any credit for the destruction of Jericho, except for having had faith in the God of Israel to accomplish the task (Joshua 6). This battle was won, and the battle with Satan will always be won when carnal human ability is willingly subjugated and replaced by dependence upon the Almighty.

However, it was not long before carnality reared its ugly head, when Achan, a man from the tribe of Judah, took the treasure of Jericho and hid it under his tent. As a result, the Lord's anger was kindled against Israel (Joshua 7:1). By hoarding the riches that had come into his possession, Achan obviously demonstrated his dependence upon the natural riches of this world. However, the carnal spirit was not limited to Achan.

Following the great victory at Jericho, a change in mind-set took place within the ranks of the Israelites, extending all the way up to Joshua himself. This can readily be seen in the planning for the next battle, which was to take place at Ai, a small town beside Beth-aven on the east side of Bethel (Joshua 7:2). Joshua sent spies to Ai, and their report concerning the situation at Ai is recorded in Joshua 7:3. "Do not let all the people go up, but let about two or three thousand men go up and attack AI. Do not weary all the people there, for the people of AI are few." So Joshua did as advised, sending three thousand men to do battle with Ai.

Most every student of the Bible is very familiar with the debacle that took place at this small town. Joshua 7:5 reads, "And the men of AI struck down about thirty six men, for they chased them from before the gate as far as Shebarim, and struck them down on the descent; therefore the hearts of the people melted and became like water." Joshua 7:6–8 records Joshua's reaction:

> Then Joshua tore his clothes, and fell to the earth on his face before the ark of the Lord until evening, he and the elders of Israel; and they put dust on their heads. And Joshua said, alas, Lord God, why have you brought this people over the Jordan at all—to deliver us into the hand of the Amorites, to destroy us? Oh, that we had been content, and dwelt on the other side of the Jordan! Oh Lord, what shall I say when Israel turns its back before its enemies? For the Canaanites and all the inhabitants of the land will hear it, and surround us, and cut off our name from the earth. Then what will You do for Your great name?

From what we have just read, it is obvious that the catastrophe at Ai certainly gained the attention of Joshua and his followers. While it is easy to cast all of the blame for the disaster at Ai upon Achan, a closer review of the planning and prosecution of the battle reveals some glaring misjudgments on the part of Joshua and his military. First, we do not see the mention of God in the planning stage or in the execution of the battle. There is no mention of prayer and no request for God's direction in any segment of the battle—factors that were clearly present prior to and during the battle for the city of Jericho.

After the defeat, Joshua rends his clothing and falls to the earth before the ark of the Lord. Had he done so beforehand, he would have been made aware of God's anger and the reason for it. The problem with Achan could have been resolved before the battle took place, and the devastating results could have been avoided.

In retrospect, it is easy to see how the great victory at Jericho set the stage for the rout at Ai. We all have fallen prey to the scenario that confronted Joshua. When he faced the great walled city of Jericho, he realized his need to place his dependence in God. But after the victory, flushed with victory and maybe a little pride, the old carnal nature bade Joshua handle the next problem within his own capabilities. This is just as true for the newborn Christian, especially when the battle is with an enemy that we perceive as being a soft touch. We tend to forget what Jesus said about our abilities in John 15: "Without me you can do nothing."

You see, the battle was not with the people of Jericho. Had it been, Joshua, in the natural, would most probably have been defeated. The battle was with principalities and powers of this world, and only God's power will overcome them (Ephesians 6). And if the battle at Jericho was with the principalities and powers of this world, then the battle at Ai was also. This, I believe, is where so many young Christians fail. Never realizing they have a spiritual enemy, when faced with a fortress like Jericho, they submit without even giving battle. Yet the Bible tells us that our weapons are not carnal but powerful to the pulling down of strongholds (2 Corinthians 10:4). Let us understand that Jericho may take the form of depression, fear, loneliness, or a host of other problems that stand in the way as we begin our walk with Christ or attempt to step into the promised land of a deeper relationship with him. Only dependence in God and the weaponry that he bestowed upon us at the cross will successfully bring down those strongholds.

When we allow ourselves to fall back into self-reliance and fail to include our Lord and his wisdom and power (as happened at Ai), Satan will most assuredly win the day. Carnal self can never defeat the powers of darkness; only God and his plan for the redemption of humankind through the cross of his Son can accomplish this. While Achan typifies the old human nature that is present in all of us, so do Joshua and his followers at Ai. God certainly defeated Satan and his forces at the cross, and he defeats them in our own lives if we, by faith, place our dependence upon him and subjugate our humanity to his will. According to the Scripture, humankind has no redeeming quality; hence, it is deserving only of destruction. This is why, at the time of salvation, we must be reborn. It is why the old nature in the Christian has to be put to death. Jesus said in Luke 9:23, "If anyone desires to come after Me, let him deny himself and take up his cross daily, and follow Me." The old nature blocks the way of true spiritual progress because that progress is dependent upon the Holy Spirit's guidance and instruction. And the Holy Spirit will not work in an environment that has been polluted with "self." To comprehend the magnitude of the depravity of man in the eyes of God, just take a long look at the cross.

From God's viewpoint, sinful man deserved the punishment and death that Jesus experienced at the cross. When we get the notion that there is anything good about our humanity, we have only to be reminded of what Jesus had to suffer on the cross in order to save us. This should provide an adequate appreciation for the utter distaste God has for any self-effort on the part of his children. Isaiah 64:6 sums it up: "But we are all like an unclean thing, and all our righteousnesses are like filthy rags; and we all fade as a leaf and our iniquities, like the wind, have taken us away". Our righteousnesses (our very best) are the very epitome of depravity in the sight of God. When we seriously approach this matter, the Holy Spirit will clarify our understanding of the grace of our Father and his love for us.

God knows that Satan will lull the believer into a false sense of security and tempt that one into service, using his or her carnal self-effort. Prompting the Christian into service within his or her own human power is Satan's goal. He seeks to deceive them into thinking that they are actually serving God, much like the priests of Israel who sought the crucifixion of Jesus. The Evil One does not fear any work that is accomplished through human effort; in fact, he will many times even support the endeavor. He knows full well that it denies the power of almighty God and exists only in that which man, through his own ability, can bring to bear. As with the chief priest, it smacks of self-reliance, and it will ultimately result in a Christian's "Having a form of godliness but denying the power thereof..." (2 Timothy 3:5 KJV).

Reliance upon God, as opposed to reliance upon human ability, is the key issue for the Christian, as surely as it was for Joshua at Ai or Moses in his fight with Amalek. It is here that the battle lines are drawn for the Christian in the fight with our adversary. As it was for the children of Israel, it will certainly be the initial battle in the life of the believer. Whether the Christian is reliant upon talent, strength, good looks, intelligence, or anything that interrupts his or her dependence upon God, it must be destroyed. It is here that we take up our crosses (allowing our Lord to put anything of self to death), if we would follow Jesus. We will inevitably cease to maintain fellowship with our Lord if we are not willing to surrender all that would hinder our utter dependence upon him.

Relinquishing dependence in one's self can be difficult, and it may take time, but God is faithful. Philippians 1:6 reads, "Being confident of this very thing, that he which hath begun a good work in you will perform it until the day of Jesus Christ..." (KJV). Our Lord loves us and desires to have our confidence placed in him. Our part in this is to simply desire to place our dependence fully upon him and then to rest in him, allowing him to bring it to pass. We must believe God and stand on his promises to deliver us from self.

During the battle with the Amalekites, God revealed his plan for their defeat at the hands of the Israelites and, at the same time, affirmed his plan for the Christian. In Exodus 17:10–13, we read:

> So Joshua did as Moses said to him, and fought with Amalek and Moses, Aaron, and Hur went up to the top of the hill. And so it was, when Moses held up his hand, then Israel prevailed; and when he let down his hand, Amalek prevailed. But Moses' hands became heavy; so they took a stone and put it under him, and he sat on it. And Aaron and

Hur supported his hands, one on one side and the other on the other side; and his hands were steady until the going down of the sun. So Joshua defeated Amalek and his people with the edge of the sword.

Moses's uplifted hands signified dependency on God and resulted in the defeat of Amalek, but his hands pointed toward the earth speaks of reliance upon human ability and resulted in a negative shift in the flow of the battle. Only as we surrender self and allow God to take control will we ever see the victory in our walk with the Lord. Like Moses, we too must lift our hands heavenward and place those things that would hinder our relationship with God before him who loves us.

Notice that Moses told Joshua, in Exodus 17:9, to pick out men to fight with Amalek and further stated, "Tomorrow I will stand on the top of the hill with the rod of God in my hand." When Moses stood on top of the hill with his arms outstretched, he formed a perfect cross. When Jesus died on the cross at Golgotha, his arms too were outstretched. It is only through the precious blood of the Lamb, which was shed when his arms were extended for us, that we may find salvation and deliverance. Our walk with him does not depend on anything of ourselves. That priceless relationship comes only through trust in him and what he did at the cross when he laid down his righteousness and took upon himself all the sin of mortal man. "Fear thou not; for I am with thee; be not dismayed; for I am thy God; I will strengthen thee; yea, I will help thee; yea, I will uphold thee with the right hand of my righteousness" (Isaiah 41:10 KJV).

The blood/water combination that flowed from this, the seventh portal, signified that it was over; Jesus had received upon himself the sin of the world and had cleared the way for humankind's righteousness and humankind's return to the Father. Those who would believe could now fellowship with the Father, Son, and Holy Spirit while remaining on this earth and then spend eternity in heaven. This fellowship with the Holy Trinity made the way possible for the abundant life spoken of by Jesus in John 10:10. Not only had Jesus sacrificed his righteousness by taking on the sins of the world in order that we might have his breastplate of righteousness, but he also sacrificed his life that we might have life.

Life also was an option for Adam in the garden of Eden. In addition to the Tree of Knowledge of Good and Evil, which ultimately brought about Adam's death, there was also a Tree of Life in the midst of the garden. After the fall, life was no longer an option for him because Adam was removed from Eden and separated from the Tree of Life. "So he drove out the man, and he placed at the East of the Garden of Eden cherubims, and a flaming sword which turned every way, to keep the way of the tree of life" (Genesis 3:24 KJV). The life that God had offered Adam would not be accessible to him in his fallen state. Adam made the unwise choice when confronted with life or death.

In Deuteronomy 30:19, that same option, life or death, is placed before the children of Israel: "I call heaven and earth to record this day against you, that I have set before you life and death, blessing and cursing; therefore choose life, that both thou and thy seed may live"(KJV).

This choice is constantly before every person on this earth who has reached an age of responsibility for his or her decision making. Every individual has the option. The Tree of Life is continuously before us. It was present in Adam's day, and it is there at the end of days, as recorded in Revelation 22:14, and it is present for each of us now in the form of a cross standing atop Golgotha's hill. It is highly interesting that Adam left the garden, which contained the life-giving tree. Jesus entered the garden, which would initiate the events leading to the tree (the cross) that offers life to us. We, as believers, on our way to the gates of the city of God, pass through a garden wherein the Tree of Life grows (Revelation 22:14).

In Revelation 2:1–7, Jesus extols much of the work accomplished by the church at Ephesus, but with all of their good works, they fall short because they left their first love. It is again of much interest that the reward that Jesus offers to them if they return to their first love will be "to eat of the tree of life, which is in the midst of the Paradise of God." Jesus is the perfect fruit of the Tree of Life. He declared in John 14:6, "I am the way, the truth, and the *life:* no man cometh to the Father, but by me" (KJV, emphasis mine). Every time we take communion, we are freely eating of the Tree of Life, Jesus, for the broken bread of the communion table symbolizes the body of Jesus.

This life that he offers is available to anyone who wishes to return to the loving presence of the Father. While it is true that the Father resides in heaven, he is also available to us through faith in the work of his Son at the cross. He is more real than any earthly father, and he bids us come. How do we begin? We begin by doing the exact opposite of what Adam and Eve did; we put our trust in what God has said. The Scripture tells us that he loves us, and we begin by learning to reciprocate his love. First John 4:9–10 reads, "In this the love of God was manifested toward us, that God has sent His only begotten Son into the world, that we might live through Him. In this is love, not that we loved God, but that He loved us and sent His Son to be the propitiation for our sins." We begin by expressing to him our desire to be with him, to know him, and to love him.

We will never experience the life that God's Word promises until we come to the fundamental truth that he is life and that he wishes to share his life with us. Remember he was the one who cleared the way, removing the flaming sword and the cherubim so that nothing shall separate any person who truly longs to be with Jesus. He bids you come and take of the water of life freely (Revelation 21:6), because the water that he provides has extinguished the flaming sword for all eternity.

We take up our crosses by giving up anything that we see as a capability on our part for making us more or less righteous in the eyes of God, thus placing total reliance upon the finished work of Christ on the cross, both for eternal salvation and for victorious life while we remain on this earth.

146

Dear Lord, deliver us from ourselves and our self-effort, which interferes with your divine plan to draw us near to you. Aid us in our endeavor to rest in your dear Son and what he accomplished at Golgotha. We ask this in the name of Jesus. Amen.

CHAPTER 9

THE SPIRIT

God is a Spirit and they that worship him must
worship him in spirit and in truth.

—John 4:24

To this point, we have focused on the seven portals from which
the blood of our Lord spilled from his body during the events
surrounding the crucifixion. I have attempted to show that each
site possessed special meaning and that nothing associated with
the death of Jesus Christ was insignificant in the sight of almighty
God. In addition, I have attempted to point out that these portals
represented specific sacrifices our Lord made on our behalf. He did
so in order to make it possible for us to receive the spiritual armor
necessary for victorious living in him.

Before proceeding further, we should reread Ephesians 6:10–17.

> Finally, my brethren, be strong in the Lord and in
> the power of his might. *Put on the whole armor of
> God, that you may be able to stand against the wiles
> of the devil.* For we do not wrestle against flesh and
> blood, but against principalities, against powers,
> against the rulers of the darkness of this age, against
> spiritual hosts of wickedness in the heavenly places.

Therefore take up the whole armor of God, that you may be able to withstand in the evil day, and having done all, to stand. Stand therefore, having girded your waist with truth, having put on the breastplate of righteousness, and having shod your feet with the preparation of the gospel of peace; above all, taking the shield of faith with which you will be able to quench all the fiery darts of the wicked one. And take the helmet of salvation, and the sword of the Spirit which is the word of God; *praying always with all prayer and supplication in the Spirit* being watchful to this end with all perseverance and supplication for all the Saints (emphasis mine).

When an individual enters the military, he or she is trained to become an integral part of a team that has been charged with responsibility for the national defense. Clothing is issued, a uniform for all members of his or her unit. Then the new recruit is provided with equipment and weaponry, and great emphasis is placed upon training in the use of them.

Clearly, as Christian believers, we too have an adversary who is bent upon our extermination. We are told in John 10:10 that he comes for three reasons: "to steal, and to kill, and to destroy." He is obviously determined to annihilate the followers of Christ. Therefore, it is imperative that we learn to utilize the apparel and the equipment that has been issued to us and that we implement the mission plan to which we have been assigned. The Scripture is quite clear on this subject; for the lack of knowledge, the people of God perish (Hosea 4:6). The Christian soldier cannot be defeated if he is given adequate training in his defense, coupled with the knowledge of offensive strategy, as outlined in the Word of God. "Now thanks be unto God which *always* causeth us to triumph in Christ, and maketh manifest the savour of his knowledge by us in every place" (2 Corinthians 2:14 KJV, emphasis mine).

We have already seen that our equipment was purchased at a great price—the precious blood of Jesus. Therefore, its quality is unquestionable, and if employed properly, it will *always* prove successful. It is, therefore, incumbent upon the Christian soldier to apply himself in training. God has made it available through the blood of Jesus, and we receive it and use it by the power that is also provided by that same blood.

The point cannot be overemphasized: when we wear the armor provided, we are actually clothed in the very armor of Christ himself. Remember that Ephesians 6 refers to the armor that we have been instructed to put on as the "armor of God." To the observer, the individual so clothed is indistinguishable from the Lord Christ. This is especially true in the spiritual world where our adversary operates. The Evil One remembers quite well his previous battles with our Lord; therefore, the believer can take comfort in the fact that the Devil does not desire to do so again. The advantage to the Christian cannot be overstated, for our victory is assured if our equipment is worn correctly. We can hear the words of Jahaziel spoken to King Jehoshaphat concerning the imminent battle he was about to encounter: "You will not need to fight in this battle. Position yourselves, stand still and see the salvation of the Lord, who is with you, O Judah and Jerusalem" (2 Chronicles 20:17).

The military recruit is trained in the responsibilities of a soldier by a drill sergeant. This instructor is concerned with every aspect of the indoctrination of the trainee who is placed in his responsibility. His aim is to produce a skilled champion from the untried conscript, one who not only is capable of defending himself but who can contribute to the victory of the army when it becomes engaged in battle.

The Christian possesses a major advantage because of his superior equipment, but there also is advantage in the one chosen to direct his training. Our gracious heavenly Father has chosen to undertake our preparation solely by himself. He does not leave even the simplest segment of our instruction to anyone else. He could have delegated the responsibility for our training to other human beings or possibly to angels, but he chose not to do so. Even when he does employ other human beings, he is always present to supervise every aspect of our training, leaving no possibility of error and always ensuring success.

To fully appreciate the significance of this choice of the instructor, let us look at his scriptural introduction. Jesus told his disciples that it was expedient that he should leave them and make way for the comforter who would come on their behalf (John 16:7–14). This One who was to come would guide them into all truth, providing all the necessary instruction to train the followers of Christ.

The most important characteristic about this teacher is that he would never leave the soldier, from the beginning of his training to his very last battle. This One would be with his trainee, not only to direct his activities but to comfort and even tend his wounds.

Who is the One who has been chosen by God to train those who believe in Christ? He fulfills the mystery spoken of in Ephesians 3:8–10. "To me, who am less than the least of all the Saints, this grace was given, that I should preach among the Gentiles the unsearchable riches of Christ, and to make all see what is the fellowship of the *mystery*, which from the beginning of the ages has been hid in God who created all things through Christ Jesus; to the intent that now the manifold wisdom of God might be made known by the church to the principalities and powers in the heavenly places" (emphasis mine).

Paul also wrote to the church at Corinth, "But we speak the wisdom of God in a *mystery*, even the hidden wisdom, which God ordained before the world unto our glory: which none of the princes of this world new: for had they known it, they would not have crucified the Lord of glory. But as it is written, eye hath not seen nor ear heard, neither have entered into the heart of man, the things which God hath prepared for them that love him" (1 Corinthians 2:7–9 KJV, emphasis mine). Paul makes it undeniably clear that the forces of evil had no knowledge of the mystery that God had planned from the beginning of creation, for he goes on to say that they would

151

not have crucified our Lord, had they understood it. In other words, the consequences of this mystery for the Evil One and his forces were so devastating that had he possessed any comprehension of what would result as the mystery played out, he never would have promoted the events that led to the crucifixion of Christ. What was this crowning achievement that was so secretive that only heaven was privileged to know it? What was so important that it could not be revealed until the spiritual church was in place? This mystery could only be solved after the church came into existence because, according to Ephesians 3:10, it would only be revealed by the church.

Paul gives us the answer to all these questions in Colossians 1:26–27. But before we read this Scripture, let me say that I would have thoroughly enjoyed being present to see the face of the Devil when he initially became aware of the impact on his kingdom of darkness, which the crucifixion of our Lord brought to bear. He must have been completely overwhelmed and devastated by what took place. "The *mystery* which has been hidden from ages and from generations, but now has been revealed to his saints. To them God willed to make known what are the riches of the glory of this *mystery* among the Gentiles: *which is Christ in you, the hope of glory*" (Colossians 1:26–27, emphasis mine). The Holy Spirit of Christ inside every believer was the truth, which must have shaken hell itself to its foundations. The realization that almighty God had condescended to live inside all of those who would elect to believe in the blood of his Son for their salvation; *this was the universal bombshell*. This truth not only shook hell to the core, but when fully accepted spiritually, it always has the same effect on the individual believer. Of course, the result is not the same because with the believer in Christ, the shaking always has a positive end.

What had to be the greatest surprise of Satan's existence and that which heralded his demise became, for the disciples, the power that turned the world of that day upside down. Jesus spoke to his disciples, who had deserted him at the cross, saying, "But ye shall receive power, after that the Holy Ghost is come upon you: and ye shall be witnesses unto me both in Jerusalem, and in all Judea, and in Samaria, and unto the uttermost part of the earth" (Acts 1:8 KJV). Fifty days after the crucifixion of Jesus, at the feast of Pentecost, the Holy Spirit descended upon the followers of Jesus in the upper room in Jerusalem. The event transcribed in Acts 2:1–4 reads, "When the day of Pentecost had fully come, they were all with one accord in one place. And suddenly there came a sound from heaven, as of a rushing mighty wind, and it filled the whole house where they were sitting. Then there appeared to them divided tongues, as of fire, and one sat upon each of them. And they were all filled with the Holy Spirit and began to speak with other tongues, as the Spirit gave them utterance."

Within a relatively short time following that Pentecost, the gospel of grace and righteousness by faith covered much of the then-known world. These men were changed; not only had they been touched by the Lord Jesus, with whom they had been associated for approximately three years, but now they also were filled with his Spirit. It is through the indwelling Spirit of Christ that we, as believers, will come to realize the power of the glory of God that indwells us. John 17:22–23 records Jesus's words to the Father: "And the glory which You gave Me I have given them, that they may be one just as We are one: *I in them, and You in Me; that they may be made perfect in one*, and that the world may know that You have sent Me, and have loved them as You have loved Me" (emphasis mine). We should seek to understand the meaning of this very important text, requesting spiritual enlightenment so that we might walk in that victory that results from the powerful but loving force that indwells us. Second Corinthians 6:16 reads, "For you are the temple of the living God. As God has said: 'I will dwell in them and walk among them, I will be their God, and they shall be My people.'" Surely it is the awesome realization that the Spirit of Christ dwells within that propels man to victorious living. However, this must be spiritually discerned. Paul prayed for the Ephesian church. "...that the God of our Lord Jesus Christ, the Father of glory, may give unto you the *spirit of wisdom and revelation* in the knowledge of Him" (Ephesians 1:17, emphasis mine).

Speaking of the abundant life that is made available through the Holy Spirit to the believer, let us read John 7:37–38. "On the last day, that great day of the feast, Jesus stood and cried out, saying,' if anyone thirsts let him come to Me and drink. He who believes in Me, as the Scripture has said, out of his heart will flow rivers of living water.'" The Scripture explains in John 7:39 what Jesus's comment means. It reads, "But this he spoke concerning the Spirit, whom those believing in him would receive; for the Holy Spirit was not yet given, because Jesus was not yet glorified." It is patently clear that it is through the Holy Spirit that the believer comes into the inheritance, which is his through the accomplishments of Christ on the cross. It is through him (the Holy Spirit) that we receive the wisdom and revelation, which is necessary for our development, and it is through his power that we receive strength and courage to grow into maturity in Christ. God has made himself available through his Holy Spirit for our training so that we may learn to walk in victory. It is through his indwelling presence that we obtain this living water mentioned in John 7:38. Let us look again at what Paul wrote in his letter to the Romans: "But if the Spirit of Him who raised Jesus from the dead dwells in you, He who raised Christ from the dead will also give life to your mortal bodies through His Spirit who dwells in you" (Romans 8:11). This great power that raised up Jesus from the dead shall also raise up to life the newborn spirit in the believer. We need only add that spark of faith in this promise to experience the life of victory in Jesus

Just as the crucifixion prepared the way for our righteousness, peace, faith, renewing of the mind, and mental healing, it also opened the door for the Holy Spirit to live within us. Through the Holy Spirit, we then receive revealed truth. God's Word is opened to us in a manner that was not possible without him. When God's Holy Scriptures, by faith, combines with the power of the Holy Spirit within us, the *fruits of the Spirit* begin to materialize. These fruits, which could never be produced through human effort, can now become reality. The fruits of "...love, joy, peace, longsuffering [patience], gentleness, goodness, faith, meekness, temperance [self-control]:..." (Galatians 5:22–23 KJV) are so far above the capability of humankind to produce them as to make it impossible. Any attempt in the natural to make this happen will result in nothing more than futility. And any success in the effort will inevitably result in self-righteousness and pride and a stench to the nostrils of God.

During the crucifixion of Christ, there were several supernatural occurrences, such as the shaking of the earth and the darkened skies. But one of the most significant was the rending of the veil that separated the holiest of holies from the rest of the temple in Jerusalem. God had expressed his desire to live among his people by giving detailed instructions for the building of a tabernacle, where he would meet with them. He expressed his desire to be with them: "*I will dwell among the children of Israel* and will be their God. And they shall know that I am the Lord their God, that brought them out of the land of Egypt, that *I may dwell among them*. I am the Lord their God" (Exodus 29:45–46, emphasis mine). God desired to be with his chosen people, and in order to do so, he designed the building in which he would dwell, the tabernacle in the wilderness that was the forerunner of the temple that would later be built in Jerusalem. Only the chief priest could enter into the holiest of holies, and he did so once every year, offering a blood sacrifice for the children of Israel.

In Hebrews 9:3–7, we read:

> ...and behind the second veil, the part of the tabernacle which is called the Holiest of All, which had the golden censor and the ark of the covenant overlaid on all sides with gold, in which were the golden pot that had the manna, and Aaron's rod that budded, and the tablets of the covenant; and above it were the cherubim of glory overshadowing the mercy seat. Of these things we cannot now

speak in detail. Now when these things had been thus prepared, the priests always went into the first part of the tabernacle, performing the services. But into the second part the high priest went alone once a year, not without blood, which he offered for himself and for the people's sins committed in ignorance.

The writer of Hebrews goes on to explain the importance of the holiest place in light of what Jesus had accomplished on the cross. In Hebrews 9:11–12 we read, "But Christ came as High Priest of the good things to come, with the greater and more perfect tabernacle not made with hands, that is, not of this creation. Not with the blood of goats and calves, but with His own blood He entered the Most Holy Place once for all, having obtained eternal redemption." (The King James Version adds the words "for us" to the end of the verse.)

Since this place where God met man had been of such great significance, the rending of the veil that separated this holiest place from the outside world must also have been of great importance. No longer would the God of all creation meet with his children in a holy place made by hands. He would no longer be limited to meeting with his children in a building or limited to walking with his children, as in Eden, but through his new covenant, God's Spirit would actually dwell within those who believed in his Son.

Fifty days after the Passover lamb was sacrificed in Egypt, the Law was given to Moses at Mount Sinai (the first Pentecost). Fifty days after Jesus (the Lamb of God) was sacrificed in Jerusalem, the Holy Spirit was given to all who believed in him.

I like the way the Amplified Bible interprets Paul's forceful contrast between the life of the believer who walks in the Spirit and the one who attempts to keep the Law. Romans 8:2–4 reads:

For the law of the spirit of life [which is] in Christ Jesus [the law of our new being] has freed me from the law of sin and death. For God has done what the law could not do, [it's power] being weakened by the flesh [the entire nature of man without the Holy Spirit]. Sending His own Son in the guise of sinful flesh and as an offering for sin, [God] condemned sin in the flesh [subdued, overcame, deprived it of its power over all who accept that sacrifice], so that the righteous and just requirement of the Law might be fully met in us who live and move not in the ways of the flesh but in the ways of the Spirit [our lives governed not by the standards and according to the dictates of the flesh, but controlled by the Holy Spirit]" (AB).

The Holy Spirit completes the armor that was purchased by the precious blood of Christ. The armor of Ephesians 6 simply is not effective without him. That armor, as precious as it is in its own right, is like an automobile without an engine. Since the helmet of salvation requires the convicting power of the Holy Spirit, without him we could have no concept of what being lost is all about; therefore, we would have no need to be saved. Efforts to employ any or all of the armor would be destined to fail without him. Jesus said that he, the Holy Spirit, would guide us into all truth. Carnal efforts to build faith, to find peace, to be righteous, or to wield the sword of truth will leave us flailing around in the dark if we do not acknowledge the power of the Holy Spirit within us.

But by receiving the truth of the indwelling Holy Spirit of God, each piece of the armor comes alive. Peter vehemently denied the Lord three times prior to the coming of the Holy Spirit following Pentecost, but under the influence of the Holy Spirit, he became a totally changed individual. Yes, after the Holy Spirit descended upon that upper room, what had been a timid and cowering handful of people suddenly changed into a mighty weapon and set about transforming the then-known world. Men and women who had remained in hiding came out, willing to face unspeakable torture—decapitation, being eaten by hungry beasts, and some even put on crosses of their own—rather than renounce their faith in Christ.

Let us look at that piece of the armor of God that is considered primarily an offensive weapon—the sword of the Spirit. While the remainder of the armor might be considered defensive, the sword is that weapon with which we carry the fight to the Enemy. Instead of waiting for the Evil One to initiate his attack, with this weapon, we are capable of making the first strike. For many years, I saw Satan as always on the offensive, always coming at me or my situation to steal, kill, and destroy. Consequently, I always took a defensive posture. Then the Holy Spirit revealed the truth of Matthew 16:18, the Word of God, which presents the spiritual church in an offensive mode and reveals that the gates of hell cannot stand against it. In other words, the church, including me, should be storming the palisades of darkness, even as in the early days following Pentecost. But first, before we go on the offensive against the strongholds of evil in the world, we must focus our attack on personal barricades that the Devil has erected in our own minds over a lifetime. Instead of remaining at the mercy of defeatist thoughts, feelings, and emotions (e.g., depression, inferiority, despair, pride, hypocrisy, anger), we should seize the initiative and bring our weapons to bear upon our own minds, which are at enmity with God. Instead of pleading with the Lord to remove them, we need to receive the weaponry we already have been given and, through the power of the Holy Spirit, storm these strongholds. These emotions, negative thoughts, negative memories, and vain imaginations comprise the strongholds mentioned in 2 Corinthians. And what does the Bible say about them? "For the weapons of our warfare are not carnal, but mighty through God to the pulling down of strongholds; casting down imaginations, and every high thing that exalts itself against the knowledge of God, and bringing into captivity every thought to the obedience of Christ" (2 Corinthians 10:4–5 KJV).

Against this backdrop of spiritual weaponry and in light of the realization of the indwelling Holy Spirit of God, the battle in which we have been engaged, whether consciously or not, takes on an entirely new perspective. When employed by the Holy Spirit within us, our weaponry is always successful. We need to begin, in faith, to bring this weaponry to bear on those barricades that have prevented our victory in Christ.

However, to be told that I have been given a sword is little more than an uninspired religious platitude without the revelation provided by the Holy Spirit. Similarly, conversion and salvation without revelation of our lost condition and the conviction by the Holy Spirit that Christ was the solution to our dilemma could never have saved us. Without that same convicting and revelatory power on the part of the Holy Spirit, we can never comprehend the possession of spiritual weapons, much less know how to use them. If I realize, however, that "greater is He that is in me, then he that is in the world" (1 John 4:4), and I further realize, "The word of God is quick and powerful, and sharper than any two-edged sword, piercing even to the dividing asunder of soul and spirit ..." (Hebrews 4:12 KJV), then I see that the sword (the Word of God) coming out of my mouth is extremely powerful, because he is wielding it.

Worlds were created and storms were quieted by his spoken Word. The Devil in the wilderness was forced to flee in response to the spoken Word of Jesus. But remember that the Holy Spirit descended upon Jesus at the Jordan River immediately prior to his confrontation with Satan in the wilderness (Matthew 3:16). I simply cannot overemphasize the power of the spoken Word of God, *the sword of the Spirit*. When I speak the word in faith, I allow him (*the Spirit*) to use it to bring about change in my own life, as well as change in the world around me.

We are introduced first to the Holy Spirit in Genesis 1:2. The Spirit of God directed the children of Israel through the wilderness, and he is referred to throughout the Old Testament. In the likeness of a dove, he descended upon Jesus shortly after the baptism of the

Son of God in the River Jordan. Romans 8 tells us that the Holy Spirit raised Jesus from the dead. We have already discussed that the Holy Spirit empowered the early church to spread the gospel throughout the world.

The Holy Spirit was always present wherever powerful manifestations of the supernatural occurred. This is as true today as it has ever been throughout all of recorded history. He is acknowledged as the One who provided the power for the sweeping revivals of the past. The great men of God, like Edwards, Whitefield, Moody, and others, credited his presence as the reason for their successes. While the Holy Spirit is that major power source behind the works of God, he is also that still small spark of light that reveals to the heart of the lonely soul the presence of a loving Father. He is that voice from within who, through the storm, strengthens the soul. It is he who makes the Scripture live as life-giving manna; he turns a routine Scripture that has been read many times into the living Word that suddenly leaps from the page to speak comforting words to a lonely soul.

Yet so often he goes completely unnoticed for weeks, months, and, yes, even years, while all the time, he is that power that is able to make the Christian life what it should be. We must awake to his presence, for it is he who assures the believer of eternal security in Christ. In addition, he is the master of psychiatry and is capable of skillfully directing the renewal of the mind. He is well aware of every hindrance that would impede the destruction of strongholds in our minds. Psalm 139:1–5 reads, "O Lord, thou hast searched me, and known me. Thou knowest my downsitting and mine uprising, thou understandest my thought afar off. Thou compassest my path and my lying down, and art acquainted with all my ways. For there is not a word in my tongue, but, lo, O Lord, thou knowest it all together. Thou hast beset me behind and before, and laid thine hand upon me" (KJV).

We then read, "For thou hast possessed my reins: thou hast covered me in my mother's womb" (Psalm 139:13 KJV). He is well aware of every detail concerning our development, all the way back to the mother's womb. Matthew 10:30 tells us that he knows every hair on our heads, and in this day, when the world threatens to make a number of us, it is a comforting thought to know that he sees us as individuals. He even gave us individualized marks that differentiate us from others—fingerprints, palm prints, and retinal vascular patterns. He obviously knows you and me intimately, and all the biblical evidence supports the fact the he desires that we know him in the same way.

The Holy Spirit knows how to increase our faith by restoring hunger for God's Word by rewarding us with pearls from the Scripture. Once the Word has been ingested, the ability is his to use the shield of faith to quench the fiery darts of Satan, recalling to memory the perfect Scripture to fit the need for any occasion.

The girdle of truth perfectly fits, and the believer can wear it in absolute confidence under the tutelage of the Holy Spirit. Darkness, falsehood, and deception cannot abide when he brings to bear the light of the truth of God's Word. The child of God cannot be deceived.

One of his primary missions on earth is ensuring that the believer's breastplate of righteousness is secured properly. In his discourse on the Holy Spirit, recorded in John 16:8, Jesus tells us, "And when He has come, He will convict the world of sin, and of *righteousness*, and of judgment:" (emphasis mine), and fortunately, he goes on to explain exactly what he means so that there can be no doubt as to the Holy Spirit's mission. John 16:9–11 reads, "...of sin, because they do not believe in Me; of *righteousness*, because I go to my Father and you see Me no more; of judgment, because the ruler of this world [Satan] is judged" (emphasis mine). Clearly, only one division of this threefold commission is directed toward the believer. First, he reproves the world of sin because they believed not in Jesus. This most certainly excludes that individual who believes that Jesus is the Son of God and that he died on the cross for the sins of humankind. Just as obviously, the third reference points to the judgment of the "ruler of this world" (Satan).

Let us focus on the second reproof, that of *"righteousness*, because I go to my Father and you see Me no more" (emphasis mine), which is, again, the only reproof directed toward the believer. For the believer, the Holy Spirit is a constant reminder of the presence of our Lord, even though we cannot appreciate that fact using the natural senses. Remember Jesus said that he (the Holy Spirit) would convict the world of righteousness, because "I go to my Father and *you see Me no more*" (emphasis mine). Once the breastplate of righteousness is positioned correctly over the heart, the Christian soldier can rest in what Jesus has done. The realization that righteousness is a free gift provided by the grace of God grounds the heart in eternal security. Jesus's righteousness is the foundation for my relationship with the Lord for all of eternity, and this can only become reality in the heart of the believer through revelation by the Holy Spirit and in the light of the Word of God. We can take refuge behind the breastplate, knowing that God's wrath was, once and for all, placed on Jesus at the cross. I do not lose my salvation every time I slip up, because Jesus, who never sins, is my righteousness. Because it is so important to the relationship between God and humankind, the Holy Spirit constantly reminds us of our righteousness in Christ. We must be careful to keep the breastplate of righteousness by faith firmly in place. This is because our minds are trained by Satan and his worldly system, causing us to believe that nothing comes free of charge. While this is valid in the worldly sense, it is impossible to obtain the salvation Christ has provided through our own works. Without the grace of God, we are doomed to failure in any effort to obtain salvation or to walk victoriously in this life (Ephesians 2:8–9). *Is it not wonderful to know that God provided his Holy Spirit to dwell in us, one of his primary missions being to remind us of our righteousness, our right standing with him, the Father? He left no stone unturned in order to keep us near him and always apprised of his loving presence.*

It is also true that we receive all of the benefits of the kingdom of God through the Holy Spirit. Remember that Paul gives us the definition for the kingdom of God in Romans 14:17, which is "... righteousness, peace, and joy *in the Holy Spirit*" (emphasis mine). We cannot enjoy the kingdom benefits without the Spirit because the kingdom of God on this earth is in him. The three aspects of the kingdom that are outlined in Romans 14:17 are all gifts. Righteousness and peace have been discussed, and joy naturally follows as a result of the other two because righteousness allows us to bond in a relationship with the Father and the Son, a relationship that always results in joy. Psalm 16:11 reads, "Thou wilt show me the path of life: in thy presence is *fullness of joy*, and at thy right hand there are pleasures for evermore" (KJV, emphasis mine). If righteousness allows us to be in the presence of God, and there is peace between God and his child, then joy must, of necessity, follow.

As we walk in the Spirit, his fruits will manifest in us. Unfortunately, some of them develop more slowly than we would like. But we can take heart in the fact that "He that spared not his own Son, but delivered him up for us all, how shall he not with him also freely give us all things?" (Romans 8:32 KJV). "Delight thyself also in the Lord; and he shall give thee the desires of thine heart" (Psalm 37:4 KJV). If we set out with a determination to know the love of our Father and set the delight of our souls in him, surely he will manifest himself to the believer.

O Lord, give us the ability to fully comprehend the deepest spiritual meaning of the message found in 1 John 4:4—"He who is in you is greater than he who is in the world." Help us, Lord, to gain the determination to know the fullness of your kingdom, which is "Righteousness, peace, and joy in your Holy Spirit" (Romans 14:17)." In the name of Jesus, we ask it. Amen.

CHAPTER 10

THE PRAYER

> The effectual fervent prayer of a
> righteous man availeth much.
>
> —James 5:16

Immediately upon receiving our armor, Paul instructs us to pray—
"praying always with all prayer and supplication in the Spirit, being
watchful to this end with all perseverance and supplication for all
the Saints" (Ephesians 6:18). We have been provided with God's
armor and God's Spirit, and we have the ear of God. Notice that
he does not limit us to a certain appointment time but urges us to
come before him continually, *"praying always with all prayer and
supplication in the Spirit..."* (emphasis mine). Once we have received
the armor, the natural tendency is to expect to charge right into the
battle, but instead, we are told to pray—and to pray *always*. At first,
this challenge appears to be humanly impossible, and the mind,
which is at enmity with God, automatically wants to disregard it as
just that—an impossibility. But be assured that our Lord does not
instruct us to do that which is impossible. The truth is that praying
continually is, without doubt, humanly impossible, but in what he
accomplished on the cross, Christ has made it a glorious possibility

through his Spirit. At its foundation, continual prayer results from continual awareness of the presence of God.

All prayer, whether practiced during the quiet time in a prayer closet or in the workplace, is fundamentally the same. Its simplest definition is communion with God, and at first, this communication is best learned in the quiet, waiting before him. We hear him better when we are hushed and reverently anticipating his voice. Over time, it becomes second nature to hear his voice over the din of the shopping mall or while driving down a busy thoroughfare. But prayer must, of necessity, begin with learning to recognize his voice. In John 10:27, Jesus says, "My sheep hear my voice, and I know them, and they follow me." When we hear his voice, we then have the assurance that we are in the proper place, whether in a quiet corner or sitting in a crowded restaurant.

Washed in the blood of Jesus and dressed in his armor by faith in the Word of God, we now have the unchallenged right to come before the throne of the Father in heaven. The right to enter into his court was certified by the cross, and the Scripture provides further instruction as to what should be done as we approach the gates. Psalm 100:4 tells us that we should "Enter into his gates with thanksgiving and into his courts with praise; be thankful unto him and bless his name" (KJV). Psalm 100:2 reads, "...come before his presence with singing." David certainly knew the importance of coming before the Lord with praise and thanksgiving. In Psalm 22:1–2, he laments over his apparent rejection by God, even as Jesus did at the cross when he had received the sins of the world upon him. David was apparently undergoing one of those situations in which all of us have found ourselves at one time or another—when it appears that God has deserted us. As was common with David, he goes on to assert, "But thou art holy, *O thou that inhabitest the praises of Israel*" (Psalm 22:3 KJV, emphasis mine). The voice of praise draws the attention of our Lord.

Though all may seem to be going wrong, we can always find our Lord near when we find something for which to thank and praise him. And we have but to look to the cross to find that motivation to exalt him. When we come to him with praise and thanksgiving for the love he revealed through the death of his Son at the cross, the Father, Son, and Holy Spirit will hear our call. We will come to know their presence.

In instructing his disciples concerning prayer, Jesus said they should direct the prayer to the Father in heaven, and he immediately began the prayer by praising his name. Remember that this instruction by the Savior came before his crucifixion and the coming of the Holy Spirit. We now know that he abides in Spirit within each believer.(John 17:23). This should give us even more reason to praise him. Many times, we are unsuccessful in our prayer lives because we start prayer by going straight to the problems that we face. We blatantly skip the most important part of the prayer—establishing communication with our Father. It is in his presence that our souls find solace, and it is here that our needs are met. Praying without confirming his presence becomes flat and meaningless and generally consists of memorized religious clichés. This prayer *dis*affirms a sincere belief that the Father either hears or desires to answer. Unfortunately, we can be in and out of a prayer time so quickly that if he spoke, our haste would prevent our hearing him. We must learn to be quiet before his presence, so that we may sense his love and compassion. Many times, in this experience alone, our earthly problems will dissipate. Sometimes quietly singing praise to his name will draw his loving presence, and the relationship that develops will substitute for any lack of faith on our part. Just remember that he inhabits the praise of his children.

There were many throughout the Scriptures who praised God and their problematic issues resolved before they could relate them. In Macedonia, Paul and Silas were beaten with many stripes and cast into prison. Having been charged to keep them secured, the jailer placed them in the inner prison and made their feet fast in the stocks (Acts 16:23–24). And in Acts 16:25–26, we read, "And at midnight Paul and Silas prayed, and sang *praises* unto God: and the prisoners heard them. And suddenly there was a great earthquake, so that the foundations of the prison were shaken, and immediately all the doors were opened, and every one's bands were loosed" (KJV, emphasis mine). The moment that Jonah offered the sacrifice of praise, he was released from the belly of the fish. "So the Lord spoke to the fish, and it vomited Jonah onto dry land" (Jonah 2:9–10). When Jehoshaphat sent the choir out before the army to sing praises to the Lord, the Lord immediately delivered the armies of the children of Israel (2 Chronicles 20).

Whether afraid of the adversaries arrayed in battle formation against you, as with Jehoshaphat, or smothered in despair and hopelessness, as with Jonah, or unfairly beaten and cast into an unyielding prison, as with Paul and Silas, God hears and already knows your state of affairs. When we begin to praise him, even in the middle of extreme trial, we are saying to him, "Our eyes are upon you, Lord, and we love and trust you to care for us."

In light of the impact that praise brings to our prayer life, let us return to the model prayer that Jesus taught his disciples. As we might expect, this prayer also begins with praise. In Matthew 6:9, we read, "Our Father which art in heaven, *hallowed be your name*" (KJV). Thus begins the prayer to which this chapter is devoted. Jesus himself tells us to begin any prayer by venerating, worshiping, and praising the Father in heaven. We know that to focus on praise assures us of God's presence, for he inhabits the praise of his children.

In praising God's name, we must remember that his name embodies his very character; he is love! (1 John 4:16). His name itself inspires one to praise him because it reveals his undeniable concern for his children. Let us look at some of the other names that describe his character and what he is to those of us who are called his children. In Genesis 22:14, he is called Jehovah-jireh (the one who provides). In Exodus 15:26, he is called Jehovah-rapha (the one who heals). In Exodus 17:15, he is called Jehovah-nissi (our banner- protector). In Judges 6:24, he is called Jehovah-shalom (our peace). In Psalm 23:1, he is called Jehovah-rohe (our shepherd). In

Jeremiah 23:6, he is called Jehovah-tsidkenu (our righteousness). And in Ezekiel 48:35, he is called Jehovah-shammah (the one who is there—present). Though the seven names were given under highly different circumstances, they all come together beneath the cross, for it was there that the provision was made for those of us who are known as children of God to receive the benefits incorporated within his name. Realizing the extent to which he went to provide for his children, can we do no less than declare to him, "Hallowed be your name"? He chooses to be known by names that divulge his love. And though he is the great I AM, he is willing that we call him Abba (Daddy), that name, above all the others, that says to all who will listen, "I, as your Father, want to be all that you will ever need."

Hallowed be your name, Lord. Yes, hallowed be your name.

The second priority included within the prayer is found in Matthew 6:10 (KJV)—"Thy kingdom come." Once we have praised his name and established our awareness of the Lord's presence, we are instructed to pray that his kingdom come. If we know his blessed presence, it is not difficult to have faith for a positive outcome, for the remainder of the prayer simply falls into place.

While it is true there is an eternal heavenly kingdom (John 14:2–3) that is preceded by an earthly millennial kingdom (Revelation 20), both of which we should earnestly seek, I believe he is referring to the spiritual kingdom in which we may function in this life. I think that this may be the primary reason why some people today characterize this prayer as outmoded, as the spiritual kingdom is already here through the coming of the Holy Spirit. They claim there is no need to pray "your kingdom come." While I understand the point being made, I believe that this prayer, from the lips of the Savior, is not only proper for this day but also is vital. I actually believe that Jesus was telling his disciples that the kingdom would come when the Holy Spirit came upon them, but I also believe that if he were here today, he would tell us to pray, "Though your kingdom is within me, let it be made manifest—made real in me. Please,

Lord, may it be so, that I might walk in righteousness, peace, and joy in your Holy Spirit" (the definition of the kingdom as described in Romans 14:17). I suppose that if one has arrived at the fullness of righteousness, peace, and joy in the Holy Spirit, then there would be no need to make this request again.

We should call our attention to the fact that in all three kingdoms—the present spiritual kingdom, the millennial kingdom on this earth, and the heavenly kingdom—the emphasis is always placed on the presence of God with us. In John 14:2–3, we read, "In my Father's house are many mansions. ... I go to prepare a place for you. And if I go and prepare a place for you, I will come again and *receive you unto myself that where I am, there ye may be also*" (KJV,emphasis mine). *His presence is the ultimate reward in any place, and his spiritual presence, praise the Lord, can be appropriated in this life, even at this moment.*

Righteousness, peace, and joy are gifts made available to bring us into his company. While our sinful nature separates us from God, righteousness, through faith in Jesus's work on the cross, closes the gap and brings us into fellowship with him. Peace, which is found in the presence of Christ, lures us as a flame draws the moth. To anyone who has mistakenly assumed that the peace to which Jesus refers in John 14:27 is something other than *his presence*, realize now that *he is peace*, and there is no peace apart from him. And finally, joy, which comes as a result of being in his presence (Psalm 16:11), is made real by the awareness of God's love.

A better understanding of the kingdom sheds a whole new light on Matthew 6:33. "But seek first the kingdom of God and his righteousness, and all these things shall be added to you." He is our righteousness, peace, and joy (the kingdom). When we come to a full comprehension of the fact that all things are in Christ, then all we have to do is to seek him, and all that we need will be added unto us.

"Thy will be done in earth, as it is in heaven" (Matthew 6:10, KJV) Here, we have the third segment of the model prayer as given by Jesus in Matthew 6. Willingness to pray sincerely for God's will to be done requires submission of our own wills. I believe it is synonymous with saying that we trust his will more than we rely on our own personal willfulness.

It is possible to pray this prayer sincerely without a deep-seated conviction that the One to whom we are praying is a benevolent God who seeks only our good and who wishes to do us no harm. The slightest doubt as to his goodwill toward us will cause us to revert to our own devices or self-will. If we see him as a hard, unloving taskmaster, sitting on the throne in heaven, ready to punish us for the slightest infraction of his Law, then we are not apt to surrender our wills. Fortunately, however, this is not a description of our heavenly Father. On the contrary, he is a kind, loving, beneficent Father whose will is to promote only that which is to our benefit. Romans 8:28 reads, "And we know that all things work together for good to those who love God, to those who are the called according to his purpose." We have no reason to come before his throne in fear of retribution; this is true because of what Jesus did on the cross. We may be disciplined by our heavenly Father, but we will never be debased or rejected. We approach the throne, washed in the blood of Jesus and wearing his armor. We should neither be afraid to approach the throne nor show any reticence to request that his will be done in our lives. While we should always come into his presence with respect for him and awe before his majesty, there is no place for any emotion except love. Romans 8:15 describes clearly the spirit with which we should approach our Lord: "For you did not receive the spirit of bondage again to fear, but you received this Spirit of adoption by whom we cry out, Abba, Father." Hebrews 4:16 reads, "Let us therefore come boldly to the throne of grace, that we may obtain mercy and find grace to help in time of need." Realizing that he wills only to do us good, we should come as children to an earthly father, boldly and without fear. No earthly father of sound mind wants to harm his children, even when they have broken the rules, and neither does our heavenly Father. Come to him expecting to be lovingly received, and you will not be disappointed. Then you will be willing to say, "Your will be done and your will only."

Admittedly, sometimes certain circumstances seem designed for our detriment. But we must keep in mind always that God sees all of the perils that lie in our paths. Therefore, sometimes there may be conflicts between our wills and his, but because he has a clear picture of the future, his will promises to be much better for us than our own. His desire, which is clearly documented in Scripture, is to see us living the abundant life, receiving all that his Son paid for on the cross. David said in Psalm 35:27, "Let them shout for joy and be glad, who favor my righteous cause; and let them say continually, *let the Lord be magnified, who has pleasure in the prosperity of his servant*" (emphasis mine). God loves each of us so much that he takes pleasure in prospering us. We must, therefore, humble ourselves, always submitting to his will, in order to know his favor and prosperity in every aspect of our lives. Let us be quick to say, "Your will be done, Lord, on earth as it is in heaven." And as a result, we will hear Jesus say, "For *whosoever does the will of God, the same is my brother, and my sister, and mother*"(Mark 3:35, KJV).

Part four of Jesus's instruction concerning prayer encourages us to ask our Father to give us our daily bread (Matthew 6:11). Matthew 6:31–32 reads, "Therefore do not worry, saying, 'What shall we eat?' or 'What shall we drink?' or 'What shall we wear?' For after all these things the Gentiles seek. For your heavenly Father knows that you need all these things." The question might be asked: if our God already knows our needs, then why should we ask that they be met? Yes, he knows our needs, and yes, he desires to satisfy them, and sometimes he does so, even when we are completely unaware of his benevolence. However, in the asking for what we need, we reveal our utter dependence on him.

An old movie comes to mind in which James Stewart, the actor, played the role of a Civil War-era Virginia farmer whose wife had died and left him with a large number of practically grown children. I remember clearly a scene in which all of the family gathered around a large dining table, and Mr. Stewart's character began to say grace. He started out by reminding the Lord that they had plowed the fields, sowed the seed, and reaped the harvest. Then, in sort of a begrudging tone, he said something along the order of, "But we thank you anyway." It was rather clear that the character saw himself and his family as the producers of the food they were about to eat. What this man failed to see was that without the life-giving properties within those seeds he sowed and the God-given sunshine and rain, all of his efforts would have been in vain. Admittedly, without the farmer's labor, his table would probably have been bare, but we must always remember that God supplies the breath that we breathe and the physical strength to plow the fields and sow the seed. Without him, all of our efforts to do anything are in vain.

If the need is present, God will sometimes supply miraculously when we are in his will and living by faith. This can be seen quite readily in the miraculous feeding of the multitudes. In Luke 9, we are told that large numbers of people had followed Jesus in order to hear his teachings and experience his miracle-working power. In Luke 9:12, we read, "When the day began to wear away, the twelve came and said to him, 'Send the multitude away, that they may go into the surrounding towns and country, and lodge and get provisions; for we are in a deserted place here.'" The disciples, faced with the need to feed approximately five thousand men and an unknown number of women and children, devised a plan to solve the problem. It is obvious that their proposal was based upon their own carnal thinking, which had bypassed any possibility of divine intervention. So out of this worldly thought process, without consulting divine wisdom, they took it upon themselves to instruct Jesus in the solution to the dilemma.

Most of us act in exactly the same manner when confronted with the problems of this life. Instead of immediately seeking the Lord's will, we set about developing our own means of taking care of our predicaments. While Jesus, by speaking the Word, can easily meet our needs, our carnal minds refuse to seek his wisdom first. Proverbs

3:5–8 reads, "Trust in the Lord with all your heart, and lean not on your own understanding; *in all your ways acknowledge Him, and He shall direct your paths*. Do not be wise in your own eyes; fear the Lord and depart from evil. It will be health to your flesh, and strength to your bones" (emphasis mine).

In line with the subject of beseeching the Lord for our needs, I remember an event that happened during my college experience that speaks to God's faithfulness. At that time, other students and I would spend our Sundays speaking in various churches, most of which were temporarily without pastors. On one occasion, I was assigned to a church that was located quite some distance from the college. When I got home after accepting the assignment, I learned from my wife that we had no money to purchase gasoline for our car, which was very nearly empty. Ambivalence quickly set in; initially, I wanted to return to the college and explain that I would not be able to take my assignment due to a lack of funds. On the other hand, I felt that I should exercise my faith, trusting God to provide. It really was a difficult decision because I did not want to leave the church without someone to fill the pulpit. The more I thought about the decision, the more I sensed God leading me to stand in faith. I had received the appointment on Friday afternoon, scheduling me to be at the church on the following Sunday morning. Saturday morning came, and I decided to wash the car as an act of faith. I dutifully went about the motions, but I have to admit that during the washing of the car, I found myself explaining to the Lord how embarrassing it would be for me if he did not supply the need. After cleaning the exterior of the car, I proceeded to the inside. To this day, I do not know why I opened the glove compartment of that car.

There, on top of the stack of papers we normally kept in the glove compartment, was a thank-you note I had received for services rendered at another church several months prior. I decided to take a short break, so I sat back in the seat and casually opened the card. Inside was a ten-dollar bill, enough money to buy enough gasoline for the drive to and from the church the following morning. I ran to the top of the stairs of our tiny garage apartment to tell my wife the good news. After relating where I had found the money, she was as surprised as I had been upon finding it. You see, we were extremely poor college students, and there was just no way that the ten dollars in question would have remained in the glove compartment, had we known of its presence. I do not know whether God simply blinded us to its existence when we initially read the card or whether he placed it in the card later, but either way, he provided our need. I really wish I had space to describe the multitude of occasions in which the Lord has intervened in similar situations over my lifetime. Praise his name; he has always been faithful.

No matter the circumstances, our God will always supply. Even in the wilderness of sin, between Elim and Sinai, while the children of Israel complained, murmuring their desire to be back in Egypt where they ate bread to the full, God was merciful. And even when they complained that God had brought them forth into the wilderness so that they might die of hunger, God still met their need. Manna was provided through his grace and mercy.

Elijah, the prophet, was miraculously fed by the Lord. In 1 Kings 17:3–6, we read the instruction given by God to Elijah: "Get away from here and turn eastward, and hide by the Brook Cherith, which flows into the Jordan. And it will be that you shall drink from the brook, and I have commanded the ravens to feed you there. So he went and did according unto the word of the Lord, for he went and stayed by the Brook Cherith, which flows into the Jordan. The ravens brought him bread and meat in the morning, and bread and meat in the evening; and he drank from the brook."

Note that Elijah received specific instructions as to the place where God would meet his needs. Elijah was obedient, following the dictates of God to the letter. It has always been my opinion that had he gone somewhere else, Elijah might never have seen God's promises fulfilled. God is always willing to meet our needs, but we must be willing to hear him and, in faith, obey. It is interesting to note that in the model prayer, the words "Give us our daily bread" follows hard on the heels of "Your will be done."

There is another consideration to take into account when discussing our daily bread. The tendency is to think only in terms of physical needs, but daily bread also consists of spiritual bread. Jesus, quoting Deuteronomy 8:3, says in Matthew 4:4, "It is written, 'Man shall not live by bread alone, but by every word that proceeds from the mouth of God.'" Living only by physical bread ultimately leads to a hedonistic lifestyle, living only in search of that which will bring carnal pleasure. Even when the physical diet is one of disproportionate luxury, it will leave one sadly lacking in the nutrients necessary for a healthy spiritual life.

We live in a time when everyone is concerned about getting the correct vitamins and mineral supplements. On the other hand, most of the time, little attention is given to acquiring the spiritual nutrients. May we be reminded that we are talking about *daily* bread. We cannot live by eating spiritual bread only once per week any more than we can live by eating physical food only a single time in a seven-day period.

We must find daily times to come quietly before him to receive from his Spirit. Beginning with the reading and meditating upon the Scripture, we allow him time to speak through his revelation of his Word of truth. Trust me; if you have received Christ by faith in his shed blood, your spirit hungers for this sweet bread of the love of God far more than your stomach seeks its natural bread. If you have not availed your spirit of this blessed truth, begin now to wait expectantly before him, giving him a warm, receiving heart, ready to accept the bread of his Word.

Matthew 6:12 reads, "And forgive us our debts, as we forgive our debtors," and this comprises the fifth segment of our prayer. We must view this portion of the prayer in light of Matthew 6:14–15, which reads, "For if you forgive men their trespasses, your heavenly Father will also forgive you. But if you do not forgive men their trespasses, neither will your Father forgive your trespasses." As mentioned, it is my opinion that our approach to this subject will dictate our level of intimacy with our Lord. We can be willing to praise him, seek his kingdom, subjugate our wills in favor of his, and rest in his ability to supply our needs, but if we do not possess the correct attitude toward sin, we will never come into that relationship that our heavenly Father desires to have with each of us.

Remember that we were forgiven because Jesus paid our debts at the cross. Therefore, we should approach the throne of God with boldness, expressing an attitude of thanksgiving for his blessed forgiveness. We must not skip over this portion of the prayer with haste because it is uncomfortable to us. Prayer concerning sin must not be taken lightly. No! It is here that we need to camp for a spell, for, in truth, victory over sin is ours through the precious blood of the Son of God. Though we should rejoice with each phrase incorporated within this prayer, it is here that we should shout with exultation because sin no longer has the power to dominate us or prevent a close relationship with our heavenly Father.

We approach the subject of sin through the blood of Jesus, just as our Father sees us through that same blood. We simply approach our Lord by telling him what he already knows. I sinned again today, Lord, and I will continue to do so until you cleanse me from it. I know that I became righteous through Jesus who became sin for me. I know that I can do nothing without him; therefore, it is impossible for me to cleanse myself. I attest to the fact that sin has no longer any dominion over me, according to your Word, and since I choose to have this sin out of my life, I know that you will remove it from me. I cast myself upon your mercy and your grace, and I rest my case. Having done this, I refuse condemnation and guilt because I know that Abba Father loves me.

Let us look at the addendum to the Lord's Prayer found in Matthew 6:14–15. The prayer tells us to ask for forgiveness "as we forgive those who are indebted to us." At first glance, this sounds as though our forgiveness depends upon our ability to forgive someone else. Our forgiveness does not depend on anything that we can or cannot do. It has nothing to do with us and depends completely on what our Savior has already done. Only he can forgive, and only he can bring us to the state of forgiveness of others. But we have the option to go on living with an unforgiving heart or to forgive, allowing our Savior's blood to cleanse us from unforgiveness. If we choose to cling to unforgiveness, the Bible plainly says that we will not be forgiven; there can be no debate, for God has spoken it. However, in light of the fact that we can do nothing to remove or cleanse ourselves of the sin of unforgiveness, we must choose to have done with it, and trust the power, intrinsic to the blood of Jesus, to deal with it. We cannot afford to allow Satan to keep us bound and, by harboring unforgiveness, renounce a blessed, intimate walk with the Lord.

We are forgiven, and we are delivered by Jesus's blood. Receive it, and praise his holy name for it.

The sixth segment of our prayer reads, "And do not lead us into temptation." The Greek word for temptation also can be translated as trial, according to *Vine's Dictionary of the Bible*. Our prayer should be that we would be, at all times, kept from trial and temptation, which come from the forces of evil and always for our harm.

This is not to be confused with the trial of our faith, which God sometimes uses for our benefit. First Peter 4:12–13 reads, "Beloved do not think it strange concerning the fiery trial which is to try you, as though some strange thing happened to you; but rejoice to the extent that you partake of Christ's sufferings, that when his glory is revealed, you may also be glad with exceeding joy." And in James 1:2–4, we read, "My brethren, count it all joy when you fall into various trials, knowing that the testing of your faith produces patience. But let patience have its perfect work that you may be perfect and complete, lacking nothing."

Having been through a few trials in this life, I can say sincerely it does not feel good. In retrospect, I can now appreciate much of the good that my trials produced. They forced me to draw closer to the Lord, and to increasingly place my trust in him. Thus, my prayer is to live my life in fellowship with my Lord, choosing to learn more and more of him and to be more like his Son, Jesus. If this growth can proceed without my having to go through trial and temptation, I prefer it (lead me not into temptation or trial). If, on the other hand, a trial that I must endure will glorify him or lead me closer to him, so be it. Finally, Lord, since all things within your will work together for my good, then your will be done.

The seventh and final portion of the prayer given to us by Jesus reads, "...but deliver us from evil... " (Matthew 6:13). Throughout the previous chapters, we have discussed the adversary and the fact that he has been defeated by our Lord. We have also considered his method of operation and examined his ultimate goal—to "steal, kill, and destroy." Most importantly, we have concluded that though he is defeated, he can still have an adverse effect on our lives if we allow him, by ignoring his existence or by refusing to allow the Holy Spirit to instruct us in the use of our divine weaponry.

Our prayer should be that our Lord would first deliver us from the Evil One and all of his forces of evil. Second, that he would deliver us from the Evil One and his evil system, which has been established on this earth over the years following the fall of Adam. And last but certainly not least, that he would deliver us from the Evil One and the evil he has established within our own minds, which are at enmity with our heavenly Father.

Dear Lord, teach us to approach your throne as we should, that we may receive your favor and know your loving presence. We ask this in the name of Jesus. Amen.

AFTERWORD

According to John 3:16, God loves each person who ever lived and who ever will live on earth to such a degree that he was willing to see his Son crucified on behalf of humanity. The Bible teaches that he placed such potential power in the blood of his Son that when it is released through faith, lives are saved for eternity. That power creates change in those who believe in it. It spells defeat to the enemies of the followers of Christ, but most of all, it provides the way to intimate fellowship with the Father.

It is my prayer that the Lord will convict each of us to draw near to his cross and allow him to wash us in his blood, that we may be empowered to walk in him. He so loves us and desires to shower his love upon us that it would be sad for any of his followers to miss even a single moment of his blessed presence. He stands ready to receive any and all who will call upon him. Remember the old hymn, "Kneel at the cross; Christ will meet you there."

To those who seek a closer walk with Christ, remember Jesus said that to follow him, we must take up (receive) our cross "daily." Fortunately, we do not have to carry the heavy cross that he bore. No, for he said that his burden was "light." However, there is a cross we must bear. Our cross is one of surrender of ourselves in each category that God has so graciously outlined for us in the blood of his Son.

1. The Blood of Gethsemane

Surrender to his will for our lives.

We must do this, as Jesus chose to follow the will of his Father, even though the Father's will subjected him to the agony of the cross. The challenge here demands a great deal, and some will certainly question their ability to see it through—and well they should because this surrender is not possible through human effort. It can be accomplished only through the blood of Calvary. Our responsibility is to choose to surrender and then rest in Christ's ability to bring it to pass.

2. The Crown of Thorns

Surrender all of our ability to adequately provide for ourselves and for those who are dependent upon us.

By trusting in Jesus as our Savior, we become children of God, and we are awarded crowns. When we, by faith, receive our spiritual crown, we acknowledge him as the one who broke the curse of poverty, and we make ourselves available to receive his blessings. We rest in his ability to instill wisdom to discern our role in providing for ourselves and our dependents, and we rest in his ability to provide opportunity to accomplish this end. He has made us kings and priests; we must wear the crown he has provided.

Surrender to the renewal of the mind.

Realizing that the carnal mind (my mind, your mind) is enmity against God, you need to learn to see yourself as a new creation. Your reborn spirit (if you have received Christ as Savior) awaits within to assume control of your life, and the Holy Spirit delights to begin the renewal process.

3. The Robe

Surrender yourself to wear a robe that has been provided for you by Christ Jesus.

Allow Christ to be seen in you, and do not be overly concerned about what those around you think of your earthly appearance. Remember the Holy Spirit thought enough of your body that he consented to live in it.

Surrender yourself to trust in Jesus for your health.

Treat your body as it should be treated, providing it with the right nutrients, exercise, and rest. Then place your trust in Jesus for your health, remaining constantly aware that all things work together for good to those who love him. If the need arises for healing, do not limit him to any method. If he chooses to use modern medicine or supernatural healing, remember both are miraculous, and both work together for your benefit. He assumed the responsibility for the care of your body, and he possesses the wisdom and the power to perform it.

4. The Shield

Surrender yourself to receive the shield of God. Surrender the tendency toward self-defense.

Life can be made miserable by something as simple as a curt remark by a surly store clerk. If the Christian is to walk in the footsteps of Jesus, he or she must learn to take Jesus's shield prior to entering the store, well before contact with that one who might be capable of producing hurt. This is accomplished by acknowledging his presence and his ability to provide you with a shield of protection from the "fiery darts" of the Wicked One. Yes, he cares enough about you to protect you from even the slightest things that might interfere with your peace of mind. Make it a habit to remember that he is present with you when you are confronted with a variety of circumstances, and note the difference that his presence makes. This practice will seriously alter your life. Always remember you have an adversary who is diametrically opposed to your coming to the realization that Christ is with you all of the time. Stand your ground on this subject above all others. Your determination in the matter will cause Satan to flee. When doubt arises as to Jesus's presence with you, remember the Word, which says that your God "will never leave you nor forsake you" (Hebrews 13).

5. The Sword

Surrender yourself to know the truth.

By surrendering yourself to know the truth, which is found in God's Word, you will be set free from anything that binds. Remember Jesus said that if you continue in his Word, you shall know the truth, and the truth shall make you free (John 8:31–32). No satanic stronghold (habit, trait, emotion), each of which is always based in darkness, can continue to exist when the light of God's truth is applied to it. Though it may be a little difficult in the beginning to study, memorize, or meditate the Word of God, the Holy Spirit will create ultimately an insatiable appetite for it. The Word will become alive and, in time, give the impression that God is speaking directly to you through it .

6. The Shoes

Surrender all carnal effort to make yourself happy or at peace.

It is such a blessed thing to realize that "the peace that passes understanding" is available simply by surrendering our efforts to make ourselves peaceful and by trusting the Lord to create peace within us. All that we are required to do is take up the cross of death to carnal effort and choose to rely on what Jesus did on the cross to give us peace. Remember that he is peace and by seeking him the true peace that passes all understanding is attainable.

7. The Breastplate

Surrender any carnal effort to obtain righteousness.

Righteousness is that which allows one to come into intimacy with the Father, Son, and Holy Spirit. Since salvation, peace, prosperity, and mental and physical health (the benefits of the Christian life) are found in Christ, it would be to your advantage to have the breastplate in place and properly adjusted at all times. By this I mean that you should have a firm hold on the fact that your righteousness *does not* depend on your effort. You must learn to rest in faith that Jesus has made you righteous, once and for all, by what he accomplished at the cross. Then allow the Holy Spirit to develop within you a healthy attitude toward sin. God loves you, so do not run away from him when you have done wrong. On the contrary, run directly to him, allowing him to know that you want to be cleansed and that you are aware that only he can accomplish it.

May the Lord bless you, and may this book awaken in you a passion to know fully, through experience, the *love of the Father, the Son, and the Holy Spirit.* May the desire to be in God's presence become such a reality that you might be driven to return to the cross for a new revelation of that love. He waits to receive you. Remember Jeremiah 31:3, which speaks to you in this fashion: "The Lord has appeared of old to me, saying: 'Yes, I have loved you with an everlasting love; therefore with loving kindness I have drawn you.'"

Dear Lord, bless us with your loving presence, and
teach us to comfortably and continually abide with
you. In Jesus's name, we ask this. Amen.

Printed in the United States
By Bookmasters